Legal & Disclaimer

C000002478

The information contained in this book and its contents is not designed to r
any form of medical or professional advice; and is not meant to replace the nee
financial, legal or other professional advice or services, as may be required. Th
in this book has been provided for educational and entertainment purposes only.

The content and information contained in this book has been compiled from sources deemed reliable, and it is accurate to the best of the Author's knowledge, information and belief. However, the Author cannot guarantee its accuracy and validity and cannot be held liable for any errors and/or omissions. Further, changes are periodically made to this book as and when needed. Where appropriate and/or necessary, you must consult a professional (including but not limited to your doctor, attorney, financial advisor or such other professional advisor) before using any of the suggested remedies, techniques, or information in this book.

CONTENTS

BREAKFAST 8

Popovers 8

Hot Italian-style Sub 9

Yogurt Bread 10

Apple Maple Pudding 11

French Vegetable Tartines 12

Granola 13

Creamy Bacon + Almond Crostini 14

Mushroom-spinach Frittata With Feta 15

Coffee Cake 16

Grilled Dagwood 17

Oat Bran Muffins 18

Sweet And Spicy Pumpkin Scones 19

FISH AND SEAFOOD 20

Coconut Jerk Shrimp 20

Blackened Red Snapper 21

Spiced Sea Bass 22

Quick Shrimp Scampi 23

Baked Tomato Pesto Bluefish 24

Oven-crisped Fish Fillets With Salsa 25

Crunchy Clam Strips 26

Mediterranean Baked Fish 27

Stuffed Baked Red Snapper 28

Lemon-roasted Salmon Fillets 29

Lightened-up Breaded Fish Filets 30

Sesame-crusted Tuna Steaks 31

SNACKS APPETIZERS AND SIDES 32

Cranberry Pecan Rice Pilaf..32

Thick-crust Pepperoni Pizza..33

Spicy Pigs In A Blanket..34

Crispy Spiced Chickpeas..35

Sage Butter Roasted Butternut Squash With Pepitas..................36

Creamy Scalloped Potatoes..37

Parmesan Peas..38

Baked Asparagus Fries..39

Italian Rice Balls..40

Apple Rollups..41

Turkey Bacon Dates..42

Foolproof Baked White Rice..43

POULTRY..44

Tasty Meat Loaf..44

Guiltless Bacon..45

Rotisserie-style Chicken..46

Sweet-and-sour Chicken..47

Chicken Potpie..49

Chicken-fried Steak With Gravy..50

Oven-crisped Chicken..52

Chicken Pot Pie..53

Chicken Breast With Chermoula Sauce..54

Harissa Lemon Whole Chicken..55

Fried Chicken..56

Turkey-hummus Wraps..57

BEEF PORK AND LAMB..58

Lime And Cumin Lamb Kebabs..58

Better-than-chinese-take-out Pork Ribs..59

Calf's Liver..60

Beef Bourguignon...61

Smokehouse-style Beef Ribs..63

Beer-baked Pork Tenderloin..64

Barbecue-style London Broil...65

Italian Meatballs...66

Zesty London Broil..67

Pork Cutlets With Almond-lemon Crust.............................68

Ribeye Steak With Blue Cheese Compound Butter.............69

Albóndigas...70

VEGETABLES AND VEGETARIAN....................................71

Roasted Root Vegetables With Cinnamon...........................71

Empty-the-refrigerator Roasted Vegetables.........................72

Fried Okra..73

Homemade Potato Puffs..74

Ranch Potatoes..75

Roasted Cauliflower With Garlic And Capers......................76

Roasted Veggie Kebabs..77

Cauliflower...78

Wilted Brussels Sprout Slaw..79

Lemon-glazed Baby Carrots...80

Baked Stuffed Acorn Squash...81

Fried Eggplant Slices...82

DESSERTS..83

Honey-roasted Mixed Nuts..83

Baked Apple...84

Carrot Cake..85

Dark Chocolate Banana Bread..86

Fried Snickers Bars..87

Peach Cobbler..88

Dark Chocolate Peanut Butter S'mores 89

Sweet Potato Donut Holes 90

Fried Oreos 91

Lime Cheesecake 92

Orange Strawberry Flan 93

Coconut Rice Pudding 94

LUNCH AND DINNER 95

Pea Soup 95

Baked Tomato Casserole 96

Parmesan Artichoke Pizza 97

Roasted Vegetable Gazpacho 99

Italian Baked Stuffed Tomatoes 100

One-step Classic Goulash 101

Italian Stuffed Zucchini Boats 102

Parmesan Crusted Tilapia 103

Dijon Salmon With Green Beans Sheet Pan Supper 104

Creamy Roasted Pepper Basil Soup 105

Healthy Southwest Stuffed Peppers 106

Sage, Chicken + Mushroom Pasta Casserole 107

RECIPES INDEX 108

INTRODUCTION

An air fryer oven is pretty straight forward to use, but with a few tips you can really make it shine for you.

PREPARING TO AIR-FRY:

1. Find the right place for your air fryer oven in your kitchen. Make sure you have some clearance around the oven so that the hot air can escape from the vent at the back.
2. Pre-heat your air fryer before adding your food. Because an air fryer heats up so quickly, it isn't critical to wait for the oven to pre-heat before putting food inside, but it's a good habit to get into. Sometimes a recipe requires a hot start and putting food into a less than hot oven will give you less than perfect results. For instance, pastry bakes better if cold pastry is placed into a hot oven. Pizza dough works better with a burst of heat at the beginning of baking. It only takes a few minutes to pre-heat the oven, so unless you're in a real rush, just wait to put your food inside.
3. Invest in a kitchen spray bottle. Spraying oil on the food is easier than drizzling or brushing, and allows you to use less oil overall. It will be worth it!
4. Think about lining your drip tray with aluminum foil for easy clean up.
5. Use the proper breading technique. Breading is an important step in many air fryer recipes. Don't skip a step! It is important to coat foods with flour first, then egg and then the breadcrumbs. Be diligent about the breadcrumbs and press them onto the food with your hands. Because the air fryer has a powerful fan as part of its mechanism, breading can sometimes blow off the food. Pressing those crumbs on firmly will help the breading adhere.

WHILE YOU ARE AIR-FRYING

1. If you're cooking very fatty foods, add a little water to the drip pan below the basket tray to help prevent grease from getting too hot and smoking.
2. Don't overcrowd the mesh tray, but cook foods on one layer instead. I can't stress this enough. It's tempting to try to cook more at one time, but over-crowding will prevent foods from crisping and browning evenly and take more time over all.
3. Spray with oil part way through. If you are trying to get the food to brown and crisp more, try spritzing it with oil part way through the cooking process. This will also help the food to brown more evenly.
4. Place delicate items lower in the oven so they don't over brown or brown too quickly. Foods with ingredients like cheese or pastry on top can get too hot being too close to the upper element, so take advantage of the versatility of your air fryer oven and move the tray lower in the oven.

AFTER YOU AIR-FRY

1. Always make sure the drip tray is underneath the mesh or perforated tray when you pull the tray out of the oven. Otherwise, grease and crumbs will drip or fall down on the oven door or countertop.
2. Don't pour away the juices from the drip tray too soon. The tray below the mesh basket tray collects a lot of juices from the cooked foods above and catches any marinades that you pour over the food. If the drippings are not too greasy, you can use this flavorful liquid as a sauce to pour over the food. You can also de-grease this liquid and reduce it in a small saucepan on the stovetop for a few minutes to concentrate the flavor.
3. Wipe down the heating element and oven door after each use to prevent grease from building up inside your air fryer oven.
4. Use a bristle brush to clean the mesh racks or baskets in your air fryer after each use. Soaking the mesh basket in the drip tray while you enjoy dinner is enough to loosen any food stuck on the mesh.

BREAKFAST

Popovers

Servings: 6
Cooking Time: 30 Minutes

Ingredients:

- 2 eggs
- 1 cup skim milk
- 2 tablespoons vegetable oil
- 1 cup unbleached flour
- Salt to taste

Directions:

1. Preheat the toaster oven to 400° F.
2. Beat all the ingredients in a medium bowl with an electric mixer at high speed until smooth. The batter should be the consistency of heavy cream.
3. Fill the pans of a 6-muffin tin three-quarters full.
4. BAKE for 20 minutes, then reduce the heat to 350° F. and bake for 10 minutes, or until golden brown.

Hot Italian-style Sub

Servings:3
Cooking Time: 15 Minutes

Ingredients:

- 3 Italian-style hoagie rolls
- 3 tablespoons unsalted butter, softened
- 1 teaspoon Italian seasoning
- ½ teaspoon garlic powder
- 9 slices salami
- 12 slices pepperoni
- 3 thin slices ham
- 3 tablespoons giardiniera mix, chopped
- 6 tablespoons shredded mozzarella cheese

Directions:

1. Preheat the toaster oven to 350°F. Split the rolls lengthwise, cutting almost but not quite though the roll. Place the sandwiches in a 12 x 12-inch baking pan, side by side with the open side face up.
2. Combine the butter, Italian seasoning, and garlic powder in a small bowl. Spread evenly on the inside of the hoagie rolls.
3. Layer a third of the salami, pepperoni, and ham on each sandwich. Sprinkle with the giardiniera mix and mozzarella cheese.
4. Bake for 10 to 15 minutes or until heated through and the cheese is melted.

Yogurt Bread

Servings: 2
Cooking Time: 40 Minutes

Ingredients:
- 3 cups unbleached flour
- 4 teaspoons baking powder
- 5 2 teaspoons sugar
- Salt to taste
- 1 cup plain nonfat yogurt
- ¼ cup vegetable oil
- 1 egg, beaten, to brush the top

Directions:
1. Preheat the toaster oven to 375° F.
2. Combine the flour, baking powder, sugar, and salt in a large bowl. Make a hole in the center and spoon in the yogurt and oil.
3. Stir the flour into the center. When the dough is well mixed, turn it out onto a lightly floured surface and knead for 8 minutes, until the dough is smooth and elastic. Place the dough in an oiled or nonstick regular-size 8½ × 4½ × 2¼-inch loaf pan. Brush the top with the beaten egg.
4. BAKE for 40 minutes, or until a toothpick inserted in the center comes out clean and the loaf is browned. Invert on a wire rack to cool.

Apple Maple Pudding

Servings: 4
Cooking Time: 20 Minutes

Ingredients:
- Pudding mixture:
- 2 eggs
- ½ cup brown sugar
- 4 tablespoons maple syrup
- 3 tablespoons unbleached flour
- 1 teaspoon baking powder
- 1 teaspoon vanilla extract
- ¼ cup chopped raisins
- ¼ cup chopped walnuts
- 2 medium apples, peeled and chopped

Directions:
1. Preheat the toaster oven to 350° F.
2. Combine the pudding mixture ingredients in a medium bowl, beating the eggs, sugar, and maple syrup together first, then adding the flour, baking powder, and vanilla. Add the raisins, nuts, and apples and mix thoroughly. Pour into an oiled or nonstick 8½ × 8½ × 2-inch square baking (cake) pan.
3. BAKE for 20 minutes, or until a toothpick inserted in the center comes out clean.
4. BROIL for 5 minutes, or until the top is lightly browned.

French Vegetable Tartines

Servings: 4
Cooking Time: 21 Minutes

Ingredients:

- ½ medium red bell pepper, cut into ½-inch slices
- ½ medium red onion, cut into ½-inch slices
- 2 tablespoons olive oil
- Kosher salt and freshly ground black pepper
- ¾ cup thick-sliced button or white mushrooms
- 8 asparagus spears, trimmed and halved crosswise
- 2 tablespoons unsalted butter, softened
- 1 small clove garlic, minced
- 1 tablespoon minced fresh rosemary leaves
- 4 thick slices French or artisan bread
- ⅓ cup shredded fontina, Gruyère, or Swiss cheese
- Minced fresh flat-leaf (Italian) parsley or thyme leaves

Directions:

1. Preheat the toaster oven to 375°F.
2. Place the red pepper and red onion in a medium bowl. Drizzle with 1 tablespoon of the olive oil and season with salt and pepper; toss to coat well. Arrange the red pepper and onion slices in an ungreased 12 x 12-inch baking pan. Bake, uncovered, for 10 minutes.
3. Place the mushrooms and asparagus pieces in that same bowl. Drizzle with the remaining tablespoon of olive oil and season with salt and pepper. Stir the roasted pepper and onion and add the asparagus and mushrooms to the pan. Bake for 7 to 9 minutes or until the vegetables are tender. Remove the baking pan from the toaster oven and set aside.
4. Meanwhile, stir the butter, garlic, and rosemary in a small bowl. Season with salt and pepper and set aside.
5. Toast the bread in the toaster oven. Spread one side of each slice of toast with the butter mixture. Place the toast, buttered side up, on a baking pan. Arrange the vegetables equally on the toast, then top with the cheese.
6. Preheat the toaster oven on 400°F. Broil the tartines for 1 to 2 minutes, or just until the cheese melts. Garnish with parsley. Serve warm.

Granola

Servings: 4
Cooking Time: 18 Minutes

Ingredients:
- 2 cups old-fashioned oats
- ⅔ cup sliced almonds or chopped pecans, walnuts, or cashews
- 1 tablespoon flax seeds
- 2 teaspoons white sesame seeds
- ½ teaspoon kosher salt
- ½ teaspoon ground cinnamon
- 3 tablespoons olive oil
- 3 tablespoons maple syrup
- 1 ⅓ cups dried fruit such as raisins, cherries, or chopped apricots

Directions:
1. Preheat the toaster oven to 350°F.
2. Combine the oats, nuts, flax seeds, sesame seeds, salt, and cinnamon in a large bowl. Place the olive oil and maple syrup in a small bowl and stir. Pour the oil-syrup mixture over the oat mixture and stir until coated well.
3. Spread the granola in a 12 x 12-inch baking pan. Bake, uncovered, for 10 minutes. Stir and continue to bake for an additional 6 to 8 minutes, or until the oats are golden brown. Remove from the oven and stir in the dried fruit. Set on a wire rack to cool. Store in a sealed jar or container for up to two weeks.

Creamy Bacon + Almond Crostini

Servings: 20
Cooking Time: 10 Minutes

Ingredients:
- 1 baguette loaf, cut into ½-inch-thick slices
- 2 tablespoons olive oil
- 4 ounces cream cheese, cut into cubes, softened
- ½ cup mayonnaise
- 1 cup shredded fontina cheese or Monterey Jack cheese
- 4 slices bacon, cooked until crisp and crumbled
- 1 green onion, white and green portions, finely chopped
- ¼ teaspoon Sriracha or hot sauce
- Dash kosher salt
- ¼ cup sliced almonds, toasted
- Minced fresh flat-leaf (Italian) parsley

Directions:
1. Toast the slices of the baguette in the toaster oven.
2. Arrange the toasted baguette slices on a 12-inch pizza pan or a 12 x 12-inch baking pan. Lightly brush the slices with the olive oil.
3. Preheat the toaster oven to 375°F.
4. Beat the cream cheese and mayonnaise in a medium bowl with an electric mixer at medium speed until creamy and smooth. Stir in the fontina, bacon, green onion, Sriracha, and salt and blend until combined.
5. Distribute the cheese mixture evenly over the toasted bread. Top with the sliced almonds. Bake for 6 to 8 minutes or until the cheese is hot and beginning to melt. Allow to cool for 1 to 2 minutes, then garnish with minced parsley. Serve warm.

Mushroom-spinach Frittata With Feta

Servings: 4

Cooking Time: 35 Minutes

Ingredients:

- 1 tablespoon olive oil
- 1 cup white mushrooms, chopped
- 1 shallot, finely chopped
- 1 teaspoon minced garlic
- 4 large eggs
- ½ cup milk
- ½ cup fresh baby spinach, shredded
- 1 tablespoon fresh basil, chopped
- ⅛ teaspoon sea salt
- ⅛ teaspoon freshly ground black pepper
- ¾ cup feta cheese, crumbled

Directions:

1. Place the baking tray on position 1 and preheat the toaster oven on BAKE to 350°F for 5 minutes.
2. Add the oil to an 8-inch-square baking dish, tilting the dish to coat the bottom.
3. Combine the mushrooms, shallot, and garlic in the baking dish. Bake the vegetables for 5 minutes or until softened, stirring halfway through.
4. While the vegetables are cooking, in a large bowl, whisk the eggs, milk, spinach, basil, salt, and pepper.
5. Take the baking dish out of the oven and pour in the egg mixture, stirring slightly to evenly disperse the vegetables.
6. Top the frittata with the feta cheese and bake for 30 minutes. The frittata should be puffy and golden, and a knife inserted in the center should come out clean.
7. Cool for 5 minutes and serve.

Coffee Cake

Servings: 6
Cooking Time: 40 Minutes

Ingredients:
- Cake:
- 2 cups unbleached flour
- 2 teaspoons baking powder
- 2 tablespoons vegetable oil
- 1 egg
- 1¼ cups skim milk
- Topping:
- ½ cup brown sugar
- 1 tablespoon margarine, at room temperature
- 1 teaspoon ground cinnamon
- ¼ teaspoon grated nutmeg
- ¼ cup chopped pecans
- Salt to taste

Directions:
1. Preheat the toaster oven to 375° F.
2. Combine the ingredients for the cake in a medium bowl and mix thoroughly. Pour the batter into an oiled or 8½ × 8½ × 2inch square baking (cake) pan and set aside.
3. Combine the topping ingredients in a small bowl, mashing the margarine into the dry ingredients with a fork until the mixture is crumbly. Sprinkle evenly on top of the batter.
4. BAKE for 40 minutes, or until a toothpick inserted in the center comes out clean. Cool and cut into squares.

Grilled Dagwood

Servings: 4
Cooking Time: 20 Minutes

Ingredients:
- 4 slices whole wheat or multigrain bread
- 1 tablespoon Dijon mustard
- 2 tablespoons fresh or canned bean sprouts, washed and well drained
- 2 tablespoons chopped watercress
- 2 tablespoons chopped roasted pimientos
- 3 slices reduced-fat Swiss cheese
- 2 slices low-fat honey ham
- 2 tablespoons garlic hummus
- 6 slices sweet pickle
- 4 slices low-fat smoked turkey
- 1 tablespoon Yogurt Cheese Spread (recipe follows)
- 1 tablespoon chopped Vidalia onion
- 1 tablespoon ketchup
- 1 tablespoon pitted and chopped black olives

Directions:
1. Preheat the toaster oven to 350° F.
2. Spread the first bread slice with ½ tablespoon Dijon mustard. Add 1 tablespoon sprouts, 1 tablespoon watercress, 1 tablespoon pimientos, 1 slice Swiss cheese, and 1 slice honey ham.
3. Spread the second bread slice with ½ tablespoon Dijon mustard, turn it over, and lay it on top of the first. Spread the other side of the second slice with 1 tablespoon hummus, 1 slice honey ham, 3 pickle slices, 1 tablespoon watercress, and 2 slices smoked turkey.
4. Spread the third bread slice with the Yogurt Cheese Spread, turn it over, and lay it on top of the second slice of bread. Spread the other side of the third slice with 1 tablespoon hummus and add the chopped onion, 1 tablespoon pimientos, 3 pickle slices, 1 slice Swiss cheese, and 2 slices smoked turkey.
5. Spread the fourth bread slice with the ketchup and add 1 tablespoon sprouts, 1 tablespoon pimientos, 1 slice Swiss cheese, and the black olives. Lift up all the other bread slices together and place this one on the bottom. Then put the slices together and wrap in aluminum foil so that the seam is on the top of the slices. Open the seam to expose the tops of the slices and place on the rack in the toaster oven, seam side up.
6. BAKE 20 minutes, or until the top is lightly browned and the cheese is melted.

Oat Bran Muffins

Servings: 8
Cooking Time: 12 Minutes

Ingredients:
- ⅔ cup oat bran
- ½ cup flour
- ¼ cup brown sugar
- 1 teaspoon baking powder
- ½ teaspoon baking soda
- ⅛ teaspoon salt
- ½ cup buttermilk
- 1 egg
- 2 tablespoons canola oil
- ½ cup chopped dates, raisins, or dried cranberries
- 24 paper muffin cups
- cooking spray

Directions:
1. Preheat the toaster oven to 330°F.
2. In a large bowl, combine the oat bran, flour, brown sugar, baking powder, baking soda, and salt.
3. In a small bowl, beat together the buttermilk, egg, and oil.
4. Pour buttermilk mixture into bowl with dry ingredients and stir just until moistened. Do not beat.
5. Gently stir in dried fruit.
6. Use triple baking cups to help muffins hold shape during baking. Spray them with cooking spray, place 4 sets of cups in air fryer oven at a time, and fill each one ¾ full of batter.
7. Air-fry for 12 minutes, until top springs back when lightly touched and toothpick inserted in center comes out clean.
8. Repeat for remaining muffins.

Sweet And Spicy Pumpkin Scones

Servings: 8
Cooking Time: 8 Minutes

Ingredients:
- 2 cups all-purpose flour
- 3 tablespoons packed brown sugar
- ½ teaspoon baking powder
- ¼ teaspoon baking soda
- ½ teaspoon kosher salt
- ½ teaspoon ground cinnamon
- ¼ teaspoon ground ginger
- ¼ teaspoon ground cardamom
- 4 tablespoons cold unsalted butter
- ½ cup plus 2 tablespoons pumpkin puree, divided
- 4 tablespoons milk, divided
- 1 large egg
- 1 cup powdered sugar

Directions:
1. In a large bowl, mix together the flour, brown sugar, baking powder, baking soda, salt, cinnamon, ginger, and cardamom. Using a pastry blender or two knives, cut in the butter until coarse crumbles appear.
2. In a small bowl, whisk together ½ cup of the pumpkin puree, 2 tablespoons of the milk, and the egg until combined. Pour the wet ingredients into the dry ingredients; stir to combine.
3. Form the dough into a ball and place onto a floured service. Press the dough out or use a rolling pin to roll out the dough until ½ inch thick and in a circle. Cut the dough into 8 wedges.
4. Bake at 360°F for 8 to 10 minutes or until completely cooked through. Cook in batches as needed.
5. In a medium bowl, whisk together the powdered sugar, the remaining 2 tablespoons of pumpkin puree, and the remaining 2 tablespoons of milk. When the pumpkin scones have cooled, drizzle the pumpkin glaze over the top before serving.

FISH AND SEAFOOD

Coconut Jerk Shrimp

Servings: 3
Cooking Time: 8 Minutes

Ingredients:

- 1 Large egg white(s)
- 1 teaspoon Purchased or homemade jerk dried seasoning blend
- ¾ cup Plain panko bread crumbs (gluten-free, if a concern)
- ¾ cup Unsweetened shredded coconut
- 12 Large shrimp (20–25 per pound), peeled and deveined
- Coconut oil spray

Directions:

1. Preheat the toaster oven to 375°F .
2. Whisk the egg white(s) and seasoning blend in a bowl until foamy. Add the shrimp and toss well to coat evenly.
3. Mix the bread crumbs and coconut on a dinner plate until well combined. Use kitchen tongs to pick up a shrimp, letting the excess egg white mixture slip back into the rest. Set the shrimp in the bread-crumb mixture. Turn several times to coat evenly and thoroughly. Set on a cutting board and continue coating the remainder of the shrimp.
4. Lightly coat all the shrimp on both sides with the coconut oil spray. Set them in the air fryer oven in one layer with as much space between them as possible. (You can even stand some up along the air fryer oven's wall in some models.) Air-fry undisturbed for 6 minutes, or until the coating is lightly browned. If the air fryer oven is at 360°F, you may need to add 2 minutes to the cooking time.
5. Use clean kitchen tongs to transfer the shrimp to a wire rack. Cool for only a minute or two before serving.

Blackened Red Snapper

Servings: 4
Cooking Time: 8 Minutes

Ingredients:
- 1½ teaspoons black pepper
- ¼ teaspoon thyme
- ¼ teaspoon garlic powder
- ⅛ teaspoon cayenne pepper
- 1 teaspoon olive oil
- 4 4-ounce red snapper fillet portions, skin on
- 4 thin slices lemon
- cooking spray

Directions:
1. Mix the spices and oil together to make a paste. Rub into both sides of the fish.
2. Spray air fryer oven with nonstick cooking spray and lay snapper steaks in air fryer oven, skin-side down.
3. Place a lemon slice on each piece of fish.
4. Air-fry at 390°F for 8 minutes. The fish will not flake when done, but it should be white through the center.

Spiced Sea Bass

Servings: 4
Cooking Time: 25 Minutes

Ingredients:

- Brushing mixture:
- 2 tablespoons lemon juice
- 1 tablespoon chopped fresh parsley
- 2 garlic cloves, minced
- 2 6-ounce sea bass fillets, approximately 1 inch thick
- Spice mixture:
- 2 teaspoons paprika
- 2 teaspoons ground cumin
- 1 teaspoon allspice
- 2 teaspoons garlic powder
- Pinch of cayenne
- Salt to taste

Directions:

1. Combine the brushing mixture ingredients in a small bowl, mixing well. Place the fillets on a plate or platter.
2. Brush the fillets on both sides with the brushing mixture. Let stand at room temperature for 10 minutes.
3. Combine the spice mixture ingredients in a small bowl, mixing well. Transfer to a plate and press the fillets into the spice mixture to coat well. Transfer the fillets to an oiled or nonstick 8½ x 8½ x 2-inch square baking (cake) pan.
4. BROIL for 15 minutes, or until the fish flakes easily with a fork.

Quick Shrimp Scampi

Servings: 2
Cooking Time: 5 Minutes

Ingredients:
- 16 to 20 raw large shrimp, peeled, deveined and tails removed
- ½ cup white wine
- freshly ground black pepper
- ¼ cup + 1 tablespoon butter, divided
- 1 clove garlic, sliced
- 1 teaspoon olive oil
- salt, to taste
- juice of ½ lemon, to taste
- ¼ cup chopped fresh parsley

Directions:
1. Start by marinating the shrimp in the white wine and freshly ground black pepper for at least 30 minutes, or as long as 2 hours in the refrigerator.
2. Preheat the toaster oven to 400°F.
3. Melt ¼ cup of butter in a small saucepan on the stovetop. Add the garlic and let the butter simmer, but be sure to not let it burn.
4. Pour the shrimp and marinade into the air fryer oven, letting the marinade drain through to the bottom drawer. Drizzle the olive oil on the shrimp and season well with salt. Air-fry at 400°F for 3 minutes. Turn the shrimp over and pour the garlic butter over the shrimp. Air-fry for another 2 minutes.
5. Remove the shrimp from the air fryer oven and transfer them to a bowl. Squeeze lemon juice over all the shrimp and toss with the chopped parsley and remaining tablespoon of butter. Season to taste with salt and serve immediately.

Baked Tomato Pesto Bluefish

Servings: 2
Cooking Time: 23 Minutes

Ingredients:

- 2 plum tomatoes
- 2 tablespoons tomato paste
- ¼ cup fresh basil leaves
- 1 tablespoon olive oil
- 2 garlic cloves
- 2 tablespoons pine nuts
- ¼ cup grated Parmesan cheese
- 1 teaspoon dried oregano
- Salt to taste
- 2 6-ounce bluefish fillets

Directions:

1. Preheat the toaster oven to 400° F.
2. Process the pesto ingredients in a blender or food processor until smooth.
3. Place the bluefish fillets in an oiled or nonstick 8½ × 8½ × 2-inch square baking (cake) pan.
4. BAKE, covered, for 15 minutes, or until the fish flakes with a fork. Remove from the oven, uncover, and spread the pesto mixture on both sides of the fillets.
5. BROIL, uncovered, for 8 minutes, or until the pesto is lightly browned.

Oven-crisped Fish Fillets With Salsa

Servings: 4
Cooking Time: 14 Minutes

Ingredients:

- Coating ingredients:
- 1 cup cornmeal
- 1 teaspoon garlic powder
- 1 teaspoon ground cumin
- 1 teaspoon paprika
- Salt to taste
- 4 6-ounce fish fillets, approximately
- ¼ to ½ inch thick
- 2 tablespoons vegetable oil

Directions:

1. Combine the coating ingredients in a small bowl, blending well. Transfer to a large plate, spreading evenly over the surface. Brush the fillets with vegetable oil and press both sides of each fillet into the coating.
2. BROIL an oiled or nonstick 8½ × 8½ × 2-inch square baking (cake) pan for 1 or 2 minutes to preheat. Remove the pan and place the fillets in the hot pan, laying them flat.
3. BROIL for 7 minutes, then remove the pan from the oven and carefully turn the fillets with a spatula. Broil for another 7 minutes, or until the fish flakes easily with a fork and the coating is crisped to your preference. Serve immediately.

Crunchy Clam Strips

Servings: 3
Cooking Time: 8 Minutes

Ingredients:
- ½ pound Clam strips, drained
- 1 Large egg, well beaten
- ½ cup All-purpose flour
- ½ cup Yellow cornmeal
- 1½ teaspoons Table salt
- 1½ teaspoons Ground black pepper
- Up to ¾ teaspoon Cayenne
- Vegetable oil spray

Directions:
1. Preheat the toaster oven to 400°F.
2. Toss the clam strips and beaten egg in a bowl until the clams are well coated.
3. Mix the flour, cornmeal, salt, pepper, and cayenne in a large zip-closed plastic bag until well combined. Using a flatware fork or small kitchen tongs, lift the clam strips one by one out of the egg, letting any excess egg slip back into the rest. Put the strips in the bag with the flour mixture. Once all the strips are in the bag, seal it   until the strips are well coated.
4. Use kitchen tongs to pick out the clam strips and lay them on a cutting board (leaving any extra flour mixture in the bag to be discarded). Coat the strips on both sides with vegetable oil spray.
5. When the machine is at temperature, spread the clam strips in the air fryer oven in one layer. They may touch in places, but try to leave as much air space as possible around them. Air-fry undisturbed for 8 minutes, or until brown and crunchy.
6. Gently dump the contents of the air fryer oven onto a serving platter. Cool for just a minute or two before serving hot.

Mediterranean Baked Fish

Servings: 4
Cooking Time: 25 Minutes

Ingredients:

- Baking mixture:
- 1 tablespoon olive oil
- 2 tablespoons tomato paste
- 3 plum tomatoes, chopped
- 2 garlic cloves, minced
- 2 tablespoons capers
- 2 tablespoons pitted and chopped black olives
- 2 tablespoons chopped fresh basil leaves
- 2 tablespoons chopped fresh parsley
- 4 6-ounce fish fillets (red snapper, cod, whiting, sole, or mackerel)

Directions:

1. Preheat the toaster oven to 350° F.
2. Combine the baking mixture ingredients in a small bowl. Set aside.
3. Layer the fillets in an oiled or nonstick 8½ × 8½ × 2-inch square baking (cake) pan, overlapping them if necessary, and spoon the baking mixture over the fish.
4. BAKE, covered, for 25 minutes, or until the fish flakes easily with a fork.

Stuffed Baked Red Snapper

Servings: 2
Cooking Time: 30 Minutes

Ingredients:
- Stuffing mixture:
- 12 medium shrimp, cooked, peeled, and chopped
- 2 tablespoons multigrain bread crumbs
- 1 teaspoon anchovy paste
- ¼ teaspoon paprika
- Salt to taste
- 2 6-ounce red snapper fillets
- 1 egg
- ½ cup fat-free half-and-half
- 2 tablespoons cooking sherry

Directions:
1. Preheat the toaster oven to 350° F.
2. Combine all the stuffing mixture ingredients in a medium bowl and place a mound of mixture on one end of each fillet. Fold over the other fillet end, skewering the edge with toothpicks.
3. Place the rolled fillets in an oiled or nonstick 8½ × 8½ × 2-inch square baking (cake) pan.
4. Whisk the egg in a small bowl until light in color, then whisk in the half-and-half and sherry. Pour over the fillets. Cover the pan with aluminum foil.
5. BAKE for 30 minutes.

Lemon-roasted Salmon Fillets

Servings: 3

Cooking Time: 7 Minutes

Ingredients:

- 3 6-ounce skin-on salmon fillets
- Olive oil spray
- 9 Very thin lemon slices
- ¾ teaspoon Ground black pepper
- ¼ teaspoon Table salt

Directions:

1. Preheat the toaster oven to 400°F.
2. Generously coat the skin of each of the fillets with olive oil spray. Set the fillets skin side down on your work surface. Place three overlapping lemon slices down the length of each salmon fillet. Sprinkle them with the pepper and salt. Coat lightly with olive oil spray.
3. Use a nonstick-safe spatula to transfer the fillets one by one to the air fryer oven, leaving as much air space between them as possible. Air-fry undisturbed for 7 minutes, or until cooked through.
4. Use a nonstick-safe spatula to transfer the fillets to serving plates. Cool for only a minute or two before serving.

Lightened-up Breaded Fish Filets

Servings: 4
Cooking Time: 10 Minutes

Ingredients:
- ½ cup all-purpose flour
- ½ teaspoon cayenne pepper
- 1 teaspoon garlic powder
- ½ teaspoon black pepper
- ¼ teaspoon salt
- 2 eggs, whisked
- 1½ cups panko breadcrumbs
- 1 pound boneless white fish filets
- 1 cup tartar sauce
- 1 lemon, sliced into wedges

Directions:
1. In a medium bowl, mix the flour, cayenne pepper, garlic powder, pepper, and salt.
2. In a shallow dish, place the eggs.
3. In a third dish, place the breadcrumbs.
4. Cover the fish in the flour, dip them in the egg, and coat them with panko. Repeat until all fish are covered in the breading.
5. Liberally spray the metal trivet that fits inside the air fryer oven with olive oil mist. Place the fish onto the trivet, leaving space between the filets to flip. Air-fry for 5 minutes, flip the fish, and cook another 5 minutes. Repeat until all the fish is cooked.
6. Serve warm with tartar sauce and lemon wedges.

Sesame-crusted Tuna Steaks

Servings: 3
Cooking Time: 13 Minutes

Ingredients:

- ½ cup Sesame seeds, preferably a blend of white and black
- 1½ tablespoons Toasted sesame oil
- 3 6-ounce skinless tuna steaks

Directions:

1. Preheat the toaster oven to 400°F.
2. Pour the sesame seeds on a dinner plate. Use ½ tablespoon of the sesame oil as a rub on both sides and the edges of a tuna steak. Set it in the sesame seeds, then turn it several times, pressing gently, to create an even coating of the seeds, including around the steak's edge. Set aside and continue coating the remaining steak(s).
3. When the machine is at temperature, set the steaks in the air fryer oven with as much air space between them as possible. Air-fry undisturbed for 10 minutes for medium-rare (not USDA-approved), or 12 to 13 minutes for cooked through (USDA-approved).
4. Use a nonstick-safe spatula to transfer the steaks to serving plates. Serve hot.

SNACKS APPETIZERS AND SIDES

Cranberry Pecan Rice Pilaf

Servings: 8
Cooking Time: 75 Minutes

Ingredients:
- Nonstick cooking spray
- 2 tablespoons unsalted butter
- 1 shallot, chopped
- ⅔ cup long-grain brown rice, rinsed and drained
- ¼ cup chopped pecans
- 1 (14.5-ounce) can reduced-sodium chicken broth
- ½ cup dried sweetened cranberries
- 2 tablespoons minced fresh flat-leaf (Italian) parsley
- 1 tablespoon minced fresh rosemary leaves or 1 teaspoon dried rosemary leaves, crumbled
- Kosher salt and freshly ground black pepper

Directions:
1. Preheat the toaster oven to 375°F. Spray a 2-quart casserole with nonstick cooking spray.
2. Melt the butter in a large skillet over medium-high heat. Add the shallot and cook, stirring frequently, for 3 minutes. Stir in the rice and cook, stirring frequently, until the rice is beginning to toast. Stir in the pecans and cook until the rice is golden brown and the pecans are toasted. Stir in the broth and ⅓ cup water. Heat until it just begins to boil. Remove from the heat and stir in the cranberries, parsley, and rosemary. Season with salt and pepper. Spoon the rice mixture into the prepared casserole dish.
3. Cover and bake for 70 to 75 minutes or until the rice is tender.

Thick-crust Pepperoni Pizza

Servings: 2
Cooking Time: 10 Minutes

Ingredients:

- 10 ounces Purchased fresh pizza dough (not a prebaked crust)
- Olive oil spray
- ¼ cup Purchased pizza sauce
- 10 slices Sliced pepperoni
- ⅓ cup Purchased shredded Italian 3- or 4-cheese blend

Directions:

1. Preheat the toaster oven to 400°F.
2. Generously coat the inside of a 6-inch round cake pan for a small air fryer oven, a 7-inch round cake pan for a medium air fryer oven, or an 8-inch round cake pan for a large model with olive oil spray.
3. Set the dough in the pan and press it to fill the bottom in an even, thick layer. Spread the sauce over the dough, then top with the pepperoni and cheese.
4. When the machine is at temperature, set the pan in the air fryer oven and air-fry undisturbed for 10 minutes, or until puffed, brown, and bubbling.
5. Use kitchen tongs to transfer the cake pan to a wire rack. Cool for only a minute or so. Use a spatula to loosen the pizza from the pan and lift it out and onto the rack. Continue cooling for a few minutes before cutting into wedges to serve.

Spicy Pigs In A Blanket

Servings: 20
Cooking Time: 15 Minutes

Ingredients:

- 6 tablespoons unsalted butter, melted
- 1 teaspoon poppy seeds
- 1 teaspoon dry minced onion
- ½ teaspoon granulated garlic
- ½ teaspoon dry mustard
- ¼ teaspoon red pepper flakes
- 1 (8-ounce) tube refrigerated crescent dough sheets
- 1 (12-ounce) package cocktail smoked sausages

Directions:

1. Combine the butter, poppy seeds, onion, garlic, dry mustard, and red pepper flakes in a small bowl.
2. Lightly flour a clean surface and unroll the crescent roll sheet. Cut the sheet in half down the center, then cut those pieces in half the other way. Continue to make vertical and horizontal cuts until you have 32 strips of dough.
3. Preheat the toaster oven to 375°F.
4. Drain and pat dry the cocktail sausages using paper towels. Wrap each sausage in a strip of dough. Place about half on a 12 x 12-inch baking pan, seam side down.
5. Stir the butter mixture again to distribute all the spices and brush generously over the pastry-wrapped sausages. Bake for 14 to 15 minutes, or until they are golden brown. Repeat with the remaining half of the ingredients. Allow to cool slightly before serving.

Crispy Spiced Chickpeas

Servings: 4
Cooking Time: 12 Minutes

Ingredients:
- 1 (15 ounce) can chickpeas, drained, rinsed, and patted dry
- 1 tablespoon olive oil
- ½ teaspoon cumin
- ¼ teaspoon paprika
- ½ teaspoon ground fennel seeds
- ⅛ teaspoon cayenne pepper

Directions:
1. Combine all ingredients in a large bowl and stir to combine.
2. Preheat the toaster oven to 430°F.
3. Place chickpeas on the food tray, then insert the tray at mid position in the preheated oven.
4. Select the Air Fry function, adjust time to 12 minutes, and press Start/Pause.
5. Remove when chickpeas are crispy and golden.

Sage Butter Roasted Butternut Squash With Pepitas

Servings: 4

Cooking Time: 20 Minutes

Ingredients:
- Nonstick cooking spray
- 1 medium butternut squash, peeled
- 2 tablespoons unsalted butter, melted
- 2 tablespoons minced fresh sage, plus more leaves for garnish (optional)
- 1 teaspoon honey
- ¼ cup shelled pumpkin seeds, or pepitas
- Kosher salt and freshly ground black pepper

Directions:
1. Preheat the toaster oven to 375°F. Spray a 12 x 12-inch baking pan with nonstick cooking spray.
2. Cut the squash crosswise into ¾-inch slices. Use a teaspoon to remove the seeds, as needed, from the center of the slices. Arrange the slices in a single layer on the baking sheet.
3. Stir the butter, sage, honey, and pumpkin seeds in a small bowl. Season with salt and pepper. Spoon the butter mixture over the squash slices, then brush to coat each slice of squash evenly.
4. Roast for 20 minutes or until the squash is tender. Transfer to a serving platter and spoon the seeds and any drippings over the squash. Garnish with extra sage leaves, if desired.

Creamy Scalloped Potatoes

Servings: 4
Cooking Time: 58 Minutes

Ingredients:
- Oil spray (hand-pumped)
- 2 tablespoons salted butter
- 1 small onion, finely chopped
- 1 teaspoon minced garlic
- 2 tablespoons all-purpose flour
- 1 cup whole milk
- ½ cup low-sodium chicken broth
- ¼ teaspoon ground nutmeg
- ⅛ teaspoon sea salt
- ⅛ teaspoon freshly ground black pepper
- 1½ pounds russet potatoes, cut into ⅛-inch-thick slices

Directions:
1. Place the rack on position 1 and preheat the toaster oven on BAKE to 350°F for 5 minutes.
2. Lightly spray an 8-inch-square baking dish with oil and set aside.
3. Melt the butter in a medium saucepan over medium-high heat. Sauté the onion and garlic in the butter until softened, about 4 minutes. Add the flour and cook, whisking, for 1 minute.
4. Whisk in the milk and chicken broth until well blended and cook, whisking constantly, until thickened, about 3 minutes. Remove the sauce from the heat and whisk in the nutmeg, salt, and pepper. Set aside.
5. Layer one-third of the potato slices in the baking dish and top with one-third of the sauce. Repeat the layering in thirds, ending with the cream sauce.
6. Cover the dish with aluminum foil and bake for 25 minutes. Remove the foil and bake for an additional 25 minutes until golden brown and the potatoes are tender. Serve.

Parmesan Peas

Servings: 3
Cooking Time: 15 Minutes

Ingredients:
- 3 tablespoons olive oil
- 1 clove garlic, minced
- 1 1/2 cups frozen peas, thawed and drained
- 1/2 cup shredded Parmesan cheese
- 1/2 teaspoon coarse pepper

Directions:
1. Heat the toaster oven to 350°F.
2. In toaster oven baking pan, add oil and garlic.
3. Bake for 5 minutes or until garlic is lightly browned.
4. Add peas to the pan.
5. Bake an additional 8 to 10 minutes or until peas are heated.
6. Sprinkle with cheese and pepper before serving.

Baked Asparagus Fries

Servings: 2-3
Cooking Time: 14 Minutes

Ingredients:
- 1 1/2 cups mayonnaise
- 3/4 cup grated Parmesan cheese
- 2 cloves garlic, minced
- 1 tablespoon dried parsley
- 1 tablespoon Italian seasoning
- 1 teaspoon salt
- 1/2 teaspoon coarse black pepper
- 1/2 pound thick asparagus, trimmed
- 1 cup panko crumbs

Directions:
1. Heat the oven to 425ºF.
2. In a small bowl, combine mayonnaise, Parmesan cheese, garlic, parsley, Italian seasoning, salt and black pepper.
3. Brush asparagus with 3 tablespoons mayonnaise mixture and roll in crumbs. Place asparagus on the baking pan.
4. Bake 12 to 14 minutes or until lightly browned and asparagus are cooked.
5. Serve asparagus with the remaining mayonnaise mixture.

Italian Rice Balls

Servings: 8
Cooking Time: 10 Minutes

Ingredients:

- 1½ cups cooked sticky rice
- ½ teaspoon Italian seasoning blend
- ¾ teaspoon salt
- 8 pitted black olives
- 1 ounce mozzarella cheese cut into tiny sticks (small enough to stuff into olives)
- 2 eggs, beaten
- ⅓ cup Italian breadcrumbs
- ¾ cup panko breadcrumbs
- oil for misting or cooking spray

Directions:

1. Preheat the toaster oven to 390°F.
2. Stir together the cooked rice, Italian seasoning, and ½ teaspoon of salt.
3. Stuff each black olive with a piece of mozzarella cheese.
4. Shape the rice into a log and divide into 8 equal pieces. Using slightly damp hands, mold each portion of rice around an olive and shape into a firm ball. Chill in freezer for 10 to 15 minutes or until the outside is cold to the touch.
5. Set up 3 shallow dishes for dipping: beaten eggs in one dish, Italian breadcrumbs in another dish, and in the third dish mix the panko crumbs and remaining salt.
6. Roll each rice ball in breadcrumbs, dip in beaten egg, and then roll in the panko crumbs.
7. Spray all sides with oil.
8. Air-fry for 10 minutes, until outside is light golden brown and crispy.

Apple Rollups

Servings: 8
Cooking Time: 5 Minutes

Ingredients:

- 8 slices whole wheat sandwich bread
- 4 ounces Colby Jack cheese, grated
- ½ small apple, chopped
- 2 tablespoons butter, melted

Directions:

1. Remove crusts from bread and flatten the slices with rolling pin. Don't be gentle. Press hard so that bread will be very thin.
2. Top bread slices with cheese and chopped apple, dividing the ingredients evenly.
3. Roll up each slice tightly and secure each with one or two toothpicks.
4. Brush outside of rolls with melted butter.
5. Place in air fryer oven and air-fry at 390°F for 5 minutes, until outside is crisp and nicely browned.

Turkey Bacon Dates

Servings: 16
Cooking Time: 7 Minutes

Ingredients:
- 16 whole, pitted dates
- 16 whole almonds
- 6 to 8 strips turkey bacon

Directions:
1. Stuff each date with a whole almond.
2. Depending on the size of your stuffed dates, cut bacon strips into halves or thirds. Each strip should be long enough to wrap completely around a date.
3. Wrap each date in a strip of bacon with ends overlapping and secure with toothpicks.
4. Place in air fryer oven and air-fry at 390°F for 7 minutes, until bacon is as crispy as you like.
5. Drain on paper towels or wire rack. Serve hot or at room temperature.

Foolproof Baked White Rice

Servings: 2
Cooking Time: 45 Minutes

Ingredients:

- 1¾ cups boiling water
- 1 cup long-grain white rice, rinsed
- 1 teaspoon extra-virgin olive oil
- ¼ teaspoon table salt

Directions:

1. Adjust toaster oven rack to middle position and preheat the toaster oven to 450 degrees. Combine all ingredients in 8-inch square baking dish or pan. Cover dish tightly with aluminum foil and bake until liquid is absorbed and rice is tender, 20 to 30 minutes, rotating dish halfway through baking.
2. Remove dish from oven, uncover, and fluff rice with fork, scraping up any rice that has stuck to bottom. Re-cover dish with foil and let rice sit for 10 minutes. Season with salt and pepper to taste. Serve.

POULTRY

Tasty Meat Loaf

Servings: 4
Cooking Time: 35 Minutes

Ingredients:

- 1 to 1½ pounds ground turkey or chicken breast
- 1 egg
- 1 tablespoon chopped fresh parsley
- 2 tablespoons chopped bell pepper
- 3 tablespoons chopped canned mushrooms
- 2 tablespoons chopped onion
- 2 garlic cloves, minced
- ½ cup multigrain bread crumbs
- 1 tablespoon Worcestershire sauce
- 1 tablespoon ketchup
- Freshly ground black pepper to taste

Directions:

1. Preheat the toaster oven to 400° F.
2. Combine all the ingredients in a large bowl and press into a regular-size 4½ × 8½ × 2¼-inch loaf pan.
3. BAKE for 35 minutes, or until browned on top.

Guiltless Bacon

Servings: 4
Cooking Time: 10 Minutes

Ingredients:

- 6 slices lean turkey bacon, placed on a broiling pan

Directions:

1. BROIL 5 minutes, turn the pieces, and broil again for 5 more minutes, or until done to your preference. Press the slices between paper towels and serve immediately.

Rotisserie-style Chicken

Servings: 4
Cooking Time: 75 Minutes

Ingredients:
- 1 (3-pound) whole chicken
- 1 teaspoon sea salt
- 1 teaspoon paprika
- 1 teaspoon dried thyme
- 1 teaspoon dried rosemary
- ¼ teaspoon freshly ground black pepper
- 2 tablespoons olive oil

Directions:
1. Preheat the toaster oven to 375°F on CONVECTION BAKE for 5 minutes.
2. Line the baking tray with foil.
3. Pat the chicken dry with paper towels and season all over with the salt, paprika, thyme, rosemary, and pepper. Place the chicken on the baking tray and drizzle with olive oil.
4. In position 1, bake for 1 hour and 15 minutes, until golden brown and the internal temperature of a thigh reads 165°F.
5. Let the chicken rest for 10 minutes and serve.

Sweet-and-sour Chicken

Servings: 6
Cooking Time: 10 Minutes

Ingredients:

- 1 cup pineapple juice
- 1 cup plus 3 tablespoons cornstarch, divided
- ¼ cup sugar
- ¼ cup ketchup
- ¼ cup apple cider vinegar
- 2 tablespoons soy sauce or tamari
- 1 teaspoon garlic powder, divided
- ¼ cup flour
- 1 tablespoon sesame seeds
- ½ teaspoon salt
- ¼ teaspoon ground black pepper
- 2 large eggs
- 2 pounds chicken breasts, cut into 1-inch cubes
- 1 red bell pepper, cut into 1-inch pieces
- 1 carrot, sliced into ¼-inch-thick rounds

Directions:

1. In a medium saucepan, whisk together the pineapple juice, 3 tablespoons of the cornstarch, the sugar, the ketchup, the apple cider vinegar, the soy sauce or tamari, and ½ teaspoon of the garlic powder. Cook over medium-low heat, whisking occasionally as the sauce thickens, about 6 minutes. Stir and set aside while preparing the chicken.

2. Preheat the toaster oven to 370°F.

3. In a medium bowl, place the remaining 1 cup of cornstarch, the flour, the sesame seeds, the salt, the remaining ½ teaspoon of garlic powder, and the pepper.

4. In a second medium bowl, whisk the eggs.

5. Working in batches, place the cubed chicken in the cornstarch mixture to lightly coat; then dip it into the egg mixture, and return it to the cornstarch mixture. Shake off the excess and place the coated chicken in the air fryer oven. Spray with cooking spray and air-fry for 5 minutes, and spray with more cooking spray. Cook an additional 3 to 5 minutes, or until completely cooked and golden brown.

6. On the last batch of chicken, add the bell pepper and carrot to the air fryer oven and cook with the chicken.

7. Place the cooked chicken and vegetables into a serving bowl and toss with the sweet-and-sour sauce to serve.

Chicken Potpie

Servings: 4
Cooking Time: 48 Minutes

Ingredients:
- Pie filling:
- 1 tablespoon unbleached flour
- ½ cup evaporated skim milk
- 4 skinless, boneless chicken thighs, cut into 1-inch cubes
- 1 cup potatoes, peeled and cut into ½-inch pieces
- ½ cup frozen green peas
- ½ cup thinly sliced carrot
- 2 tablespoons chopped onion
- ½ cup chopped celery
- 1 teaspoon garlic powder
- Salt and freshly ground black pepper to taste
- 8 sheets phyllo pastry, thawed Olive oil

Directions:
1. Preheat the toaster oven to 400° F.
2. Whisk the flour into the milk until smooth in a 1-quart 8½ × 8½ × 4-inch ovenproof baking dish. Add the remaining filling ingredients and mix well. Adjust the seasonings to taste. Cover the dish with aluminum foil.
3. BAKE for 40 minutes, or until the carrot, potatoes, and celery are tender. Remove from the oven and uncover.
4. Place one sheet of phyllo pastry on top of the baked pie-filling mixture, bending the edges to fit the shape of the baking dish. Brush the sheet with olive oil. Add another sheet on top of it and brush with oil. Continue adding the remaining sheets, brushing each one, until the crust is completed. Brush the top with oil.
5. BAKE for 6 minutes, or until the phyllo pastry is browned.

Chicken-fried Steak With Gravy

Servings: 2
Cooking Time: 16 Minutes

Ingredients:
- FOR THE STEAK
- Oil spray (hand-pumped)
- 1 cup all-purpose flour
- 1 teaspoon garlic powder
- 1 teaspoon onion powder
- 1 teaspoon smoked paprika
- 2 large eggs
- 2 (½-pound) cube steaks
- Sea salt, for seasoning
- Freshly ground black pepper, for seasoning
- FOR THE GRAVY
- 2 tablespoons salted butter
- 2 tablespoons all-purpose flour
- 1½ cups whole milk
- ¼ cup heavy (whipping) cream
- Sea salt, for seasoning
- Freshly ground black pepper, for seasoning

Directions:

1. To make the steak
2. Preheat the toaster oven to 400°F on AIR FRY for 5 minutes.
3. Place the air-fryer basket in the baking tray and spray it generously with the oil.
4. In a medium bowl, stir the flour, garlic powder, onion powder, and paprika until well blended.
5. In a medium bowl, beat the eggs and place them next to the flour.
6. Season the steaks all over with salt and pepper.
7. Dredge a steak in the egg and then in the flour mixture, making sure it is well coated. Shake off any excess flour.
8. Place the steak in the basket and repeat the process with the other steak.
9. Spray the tops of the steaks with the oil.
10. In position 2, air fry for 9 minutes until golden brown and crispy. Turn the steaks over, spray the second side with the oil, and air fry for an additional 7 minutes.
11. Set the steaks aside to rest for 5 minutes.
12. To make the gravy
13. While the steak is air frying, melt the butter in a medium saucepan over medium-high heat.
14. Whisk in the flour and cook for 2 minutes until lightly browned.
15. Whisk in the milk until the gravy is creamy and thick, about 5 minutes. Whisk in the cream and season with salt and pepper.
16. Serve the steak topped with the gravy.

Oven-crisped Chicken

Servings: 4
Cooking Time: 35 Minutes

Ingredients:
- Coating mixture:
- 1 cup cornmeal
- ¼ cup wheat germ
- 1 teaspoon paprika
- 1 teaspoon garlic powder
- Salt and butcher's pepper to taste
- 3 tablespoons olive oil
- 1 tablespoon spicy brown mustard
- 6 skinless, boneless chicken thighs

Directions:
1. Preheat the toaster oven to 375° F.
2. Combine the coating mixture ingredients in a small bowl and transfer to a plate, spreading the mixture evenly over the plate's surface. Set aside.
3. Whisk together the oil and mustard in a bowl. Add the chicken pieces and toss to coat thoroughly. Press both sides of each piece into the coating mixture to coat well. Chill in the refrigerator for 10 minutes. Transfer the chicken pieces to a broiling rack with a pan underneath.
4. BAKE, uncovered, for 35 minutes, or until the meat is tender and the coating is crisp and golden brown or browned to your preference.

Chicken Pot Pie

Servings: 4
Cooking Time: 65 Minutes

Ingredients:

- ¼ cup salted butter
- 1 small sweet onion, chopped
- 1 carrot, chopped
- 1 teaspoon minced garlic
- ¼ cup all-purpose flour
- 1 cup low-sodium chicken broth
- ¼ cup heavy (whipping) cream
- 2 cups diced store-bought rotisserie chicken
- 1 cup frozen peas
- Sea salt, for seasoning
- Freshly ground black pepper, for seasoning
- 1 unbaked store-bought pie crust

Directions:

1. Place the rack in position 1 and preheat the toaster oven to 350°F on BAKE for 5 minutes.
2. Melt the butter in a large saucepan over medium-high heat. Sauté the onion, carrot, and garlic until softened, about 12 minutes. Whisk in the flour to form a thick paste and whisk for 1 minute to cook.
3. Add the broth and whisk until thickened, about 2 minutes. Add the heavy cream, whisking to combine. Add the chicken and peas, and season with salt and pepper.
4. Transfer the filling to a 1½-quart casserole dish and top with the pie crust, tucking the edges into the sides of the casserole dish to completely enclose the filling. Cut 4 or 5 slits in the top of the crust.
5. Bake for 50 minutes until the crust is golden brown and the filling is bubbly. Serve.

Chicken Breast With Chermoula Sauce

Servings: 4

Cooking Time: 15 Minutes

Ingredients:

- Chicken Ingredients
- 2 boneless skinless chicken breasts 1 tablespoon olive oil
- 1 teaspoon salt
- 1 teaspoon pepper
- Chermoula Ingredients
- 1 cup fresh cilantro
- 1 cup fresh parsley
- ¼ cup fresh mint
- ½ teaspoon red chili flakes
- ½ teaspoon cumin seeds
- ½ teaspoon coriander seeds
- 3 garlic cloves, peeled
- ½ cup extra virgin olive oil
- 1 lemon, zested and juiced
- ¾ teaspoons smoked paprika
- ¾ teaspoons salt

Directions:

1. Combine all the chermoula sauce ingredients in a blender or food processor. Pulse until smooth. Taste and add salt if needed. Place into a bowl and set aside.
2. Slice the chicken breast in half lengthwise and lightly pound with a meat tenderizer until both halves are about
3. ½-inch thick.
4. Preheat the toaster oven to 430°F.
5. Line the food tray with foil, then place the chicken breasts on the tray. Drizzle chicken with olive oil and season with salt and pepper.
6. Insert the food tray at top position in the preheated oven.
7. Select the Air Fry function, adjust time to 15 minutes, and press Start/Pause.
8. Remove when the chicken breast reaches an internal temperature of 160°F. Allow the chicken to rest for 5 minutes.
9. Brush the chermoula sauce over the chicken, or serve chicken with chermoula sauce on the side.

Harissa Lemon Whole Chicken

Servings: 6
Cooking Time: 60 Minutes

Ingredients:

- 2 teaspoons kosher salt
- ½ teaspoon freshly ground black pepper
- ½ teaspoon ground cumin
- 2 garlic cloves
- 6 tablespoons harissa paste
- ½ lemon, juiced
- 1 whole lemon, zested
- 1 (5 pound) whole chicken

Directions:

1. Place salt, pepper, cumin, garlic cloves, harissa paste, lemon juice, and lemon zest in a food processor and pulse until they form a smooth puree.
2. Rub the puree all over the chicken, especially inside the cavity, and cover with plastic wrap.
3. Marinate for 1 hour at room temperature.
4. Preheat the toaster oven to 350°F.
5. Place the marinated chicken on the food tray, then insert the tray at low position in the preheated oven.
6. Select the Roast function, then press Start/Pause.
7. Remove when done, tent chicken with foil, and allow it to rest for 20 minutes before serving.

Fried Chicken

Servings: 4
Cooking Time: 40 Minutes

Ingredients:

- 12 skin-on chicken drumsticks
- 1 cup buttermilk
- 1½ cups all-purpose flour
- 1 tablespoon smoked paprika
- ¾ teaspoon celery salt
- ¾ teaspoon dried mustard
- ½ teaspoon garlic powder
- ½ teaspoon freshly ground black pepper
- ½ teaspoon sea salt
- ½ teaspoon dried thyme
- ¼ teaspoon dried oregano
- 4 large eggs
- Oil spray (hand-pumped)

Directions:

1. Place the chicken and buttermilk in a medium bowl, cover, and refrigerate for at least 1 hour, up to overnight.
2. Preheat the toaster oven to 375°F on AIR FRY for 5 minutes.
3. In a large bowl, stir the flour, paprika, celery salt, mustard, garlic powder, pepper, salt, thyme, and oregano until well mixed.
4. Beat the eggs until frothy in a medium bowl and set them beside the flour.
5. Place the air-fryer basket in the baking tray and generously spray it with the oil.
6. Dredge a chicken drumstick in the flour, then the eggs, and then in the flour again, thickly coating it, and place the drumstick in the basket. Repeat with 5 more drumsticks and spray them all lightly with the oil on all sides.
7. In position 2, air fry for 20 minutes, turning halfway through, until golden brown and crispy with an internal temperature of 165°F.
8. Repeat with the remaining chicken, covering the cooked chicken loosely with foil to keep it warm. Serve.

Turkey-hummus Wraps

Servings: 4
Cooking Time: 7 Minutes

Ingredients:
- 4 large whole wheat wraps
- ½ cup hummus
- 16 thin slices deli turkey
- 8 slices provolone cheese
- 1 cup fresh baby spinach (or more to taste)

Directions:
1. To assemble, place 2 tablespoons of hummus on each wrap and spread to within about a half inch from edges. Top with 4 slices of turkey and 2 slices of provolone. Finish with ¼ cup of baby spinach—or pile on as much as you like.
2. Roll up each wrap. You don't need to fold or seal the ends.
3. Place 2 wraps in air fryer oven, seam side down.
4. Air-fry at 360°F for 4 minutes to warm filling and melt cheese. If you like, you can continue cooking for 3 more minutes, until the wrap is slightly crispy.
5. Repeat step 4 to cook remaining wraps.

BEEF PORK AND LAMB

Lime And Cumin Lamb Kebabs

Servings: 4
Cooking Time: 16 Minutes

Ingredients:
- 1 pound boneless lean lamb, trimmed and cut into 1 × 1-inch pieces
- 2 plum tomatoes, cut into 2 × 2-inch pieces
- 1 bell pepper, cut into 2 × 2-inch pieces
- 1 small onion, cut into 2 × 2-inch pieces
- Brushing mixture:
- ¼ cup lime juice
- ½ teaspoon soy sauce
- 1 tablespoon honey
- 1½ teaspoon ground cumin

Directions:
1. Skewer alternating pieces of lamb, tomato, pepper, and onion on four 9-inch skewers.
2. Combine the brushing mixture ingredients in a small bowl and brush on the kebabs. Place the skewers on a broiling rack with a pan underneath.
3. BROIL for 8 minutes. Turn the skewers, brush the kebabs with the mixture, and broil for 8 minutes, or until the meat and vegetables are cooked and browned.

Better-than-chinese-take-out Pork Ribs

Servings: 3
Cooking Time: 35 Minutes

Ingredients:

- 1½ tablespoons Hoisin sauce (gluten-free, if a concern)
- 1½ tablespoons Regular or low-sodium soy sauce or gluten-free tamari sauce
- 1½ tablespoons Shaoxing (Chinese cooking rice wine), dry sherry, or white grape juice
- 1½ teaspoons Minced garlic
- ¾ teaspoon Ground dried ginger
- ¾ teaspoon Ground white pepper
- 1½ pounds Pork baby back rib rack(s), cut into 2-bone pieces

Directions:

1. Mix the hoisin sauce, soy or tamari sauce, Shaoxing or its substitute, garlic, ginger, and white pepper in a large bowl. Add the rib sections and stir well to coat. Cover and refrigerate for at least 2 hours or up to 24 hours, stirring the rib sections in the marinade occasionally.
2. Preheat the toaster oven to 350°F . Set the ribs in their bowl on the counter as the machine heats.
3. When the machine is at temperature, set the rib pieces on their sides in a single layer in the air fryer oven with as much air space between them as possible. Air-fry for 35 minutes, turning and rearranging the pieces once, until deeply browned and sizzling.
4. Use kitchen tongs to transfer the rib pieces to a large serving bowl or platter. Wait a minute or two before serving them so the meat can reabsorb some of its own juices.

Calf's Liver

Servings: 4
Cooking Time: 5 Minutes

Ingredients:
- 1 pound sliced calf's liver
- salt and pepper
- 2 eggs
- 2 tablespoons milk
- ½ cup whole wheat flour
- 1½ cups panko breadcrumbs
- ½ cup plain breadcrumbs
- ½ teaspoon salt
- ¼ teaspoon pepper
- oil for misting or cooking spray

Directions:
1. Cut liver slices crosswise into strips about ½-inch wide. Sprinkle with salt and pepper to taste.
2. Beat together egg and milk in a shallow dish.
3. Place wheat flour in a second shallow dish.
4. In a third shallow dish, mix together panko, plain breadcrumbs, ½ teaspoon salt, and ¼ teaspoon pepper.
5. Preheat the toaster oven to 390°F.
6. Dip liver strips in flour, egg wash, and then breadcrumbs, pressing in coating slightly to make crumbs stick.
7. Cooking half the liver at a time, place strips in air fryer oven in a single layer, close but not touching. Air-fry at 390°F for 5 minutes or until done to your preference.
8. Repeat step 7 to cook remaining liver.

Beef Bourguignon

Servings: 6
Cooking Time: 240 Minutes

Ingredients:

- 4 slices bacon, chopped into ½-inch pieces
- 3 pounds chuck roast, cut into 2-inch chunks
- 1 tablespoon kosher salt, plus more to taste
- 1½ tablespoons black pepper, plus more to taste
- 4 tablespoons all purpose flour, divided
- 2 tablespoons olive oil
- 2 large carrots, cut into ½-inch thick slices
- ½ large white onion, diced
- 4 cloves garlic, minced
- 2 tablespoons tomato paste
- 3 cups red wine (Merlot, Pinot Noir, or Chianti)
- 2 cups beef stock
- 1 beef bouillon cube, crushed
- ½ teaspoon dried thyme
- ¼ teaspoon dried parsley
- 2 bay leaves
- 10 ounces fresh small white or brown mushrooms, quartered
- 2 tablespoons cornstarch (optional)
- 2 tablespoons water (optional)

Directions:

1. Render the bacon in a large pot over medium heat for 5 minutes or until crispy.
2. Drain the bacon and set aside, leaving the bacon fat in the pot.
3. Mix together chuck roast chunks, kosher salt, black pepper, and 2 tablespoons of all purpose flour until well combined.
4. Dredge the beef of any extra flour and sear in the bacon grease for about 4 minutes on each side. It is important not to overcrowd the pot, so you may need to work in batches.
5. Remove the beef when done and set aside with the bacon.
6. Add the olive oil, sliced carrots, and diced onion to the pot. Cook for 5 minutes, then add the garlic and cook for another minute.
7. Add the tomato paste and cook for 1 minute, then mix in the remaining 2 tablespoons of flour and cook on medium low for 4 minutes.
8. Pour in the wine and beef stock, scraping the bottom of the pot to make sure there aren't any bits stuck to the bottom.
9. Add the bacon and seared meat back into the pot, along with the bouillon cube, dried thyme, dried parsley, bay leaves, and mushrooms. Mix well and bring to a light boil.
10. Insert the wire rack at low position in the Air Fryer Toaster Oven.
11. Cover the pot with foil and place on the rack in the oven. Make sure the foil is secure so it doesn't lift and contact the heating elements.
12. Select the Slow Cook function, adjust time to 4 hours, and press Start/Pause.
13. Remove the pot carefully from the oven when done and place back on the stove.
14. Discard the foil, mix the stew, and season to taste with salt and pepper.
15. Thicken the stew if desired by using a cornstarch slurry of 2 tablespoons cornstarch and 2 tablespoons water. Add half, mix, and bring to a boil, stirring occasionally. If the sauce is still too thin, add the other half of the slurry.

Smokehouse-style Beef Ribs

Servings: 3
Cooking Time: 25 Minutes

Ingredients:

- ¼ teaspoon Mild smoked paprika
- ¼ teaspoon Garlic powder
- ¼ teaspoon Onion powder
- ¼ teaspoon Table salt
- ¼ teaspoon Ground black pepper
- 3 10- to 12-ounce beef back ribs (not beef short ribs)

Directions:

1. Preheat the toaster oven to 350°F .
2. Mix the smoked paprika, garlic powder, onion powder, salt, and pepper in a small bowl until uniform. Massage and pat this mixture onto the ribs.
3. When the machine is at temperature, set the ribs in the air fryer oven in one layer, turning them on their sides if necessary, sort of like they're spooning but with at least ¼ inch air space between them. Air-fry for 25 minutes, turning once, until deep brown and sizzling.
4. Use kitchen tongs to transfer the ribs to a wire rack. Cool for 5 minutes before serving.

Beer-baked Pork Tenderloin

Servings: 4
Cooking Time: 40 Minutes

Ingredients:

- 1 pound lean pork tenderloin, fat trimmed off
- 3 garlic cloves, minced
- 1 cup good-quality dark ale or beer
- 2 bay leaves
- Salt and freshly cracked black pepper
- Spiced apple slices

Directions:

1. Preheat the toaster oven to 400° F.
2. Place the tenderloin in an 8½ × 8½ × 4-inch ovenproof baking dish. Sprinkle the minced garlic over the pork, pour over the beer, add the bay leaves, and season to taste with the salt and pepper. Cover with aluminum foil.
3. BAKE, covered, for 40 minutes, or until the meat is tender. Discard the bay leaves and serve sliced with the liquid. Garnish with the spiced apple slices.

Barbecue-style London Broil

Servings: 5
Cooking Time: 17 Minutes

Ingredients:

- ¾ teaspoon Mild smoked paprika
- ¾ teaspoon Dried oregano
- ¾ teaspoon Table salt
- ¾ teaspoon Ground black pepper
- ¼ teaspoon Garlic powder
- ¼ teaspoon Onion powder
- 1½ pounds Beef London broil (in one piece)
- Olive oil spray

Directions:

1. Preheat the toaster oven to 400°F.
2. Mix the smoked paprika, oregano, salt, pepper, garlic powder, and onion powder in a small bowl until uniform.
3. Pat and rub this mixture across all surfaces of the beef. Lightly coat the beef on all sides with olive oil spray.
4. When the machine is at temperature, lay the London broil flat in the air fryer oven and air-fry undisturbed for 8 minutes for the small batch, 10 minutes for the medium batch, or 12 minutes for the large batch for medium-rare, until an instant-read meat thermometer inserted into the center of the meat registers 130°F (not USDA-approved). Add 1, 2, or 3 minutes, respectively (based on the size of the cut) for medium, until an instant-read meat thermometer registers 135°F (not USDA-approved). Or add 3, 4, or 5 minutes respectively for medium, until an instant-read meat thermometer registers 145°F (USDA-approved).
5. Use kitchen tongs to transfer the London broil to a cutting board. Let the meat rest for 10 minutes. It needs a long time for the juices to be reincorporated into the meat's fibers. Carve it against the grain into very thin (less than ¼-inch-thick) slices to serve.

Italian Meatballs

Servings: 4
Cooking Time: 12 Minutes

Ingredients:

- 12 ounces lean ground beef
- 4 ounces Italian sausage, casing removed
- ½ cup breadcrumbs
- 1 cup grated Parmesan cheese
- 1 egg
- 2 tablespoons milk
- 2 teaspoons Italian seasoning
- ½ teaspoon onion powder
- ½ teaspoon garlic powder
- Pinch of red pepper flakes

Directions:

1. In a large bowl, place all the ingredients and mix well. Roll out 24 meatballs.
2. Preheat the toaster oven to 360°F.
3. Place the meatballs in the air fryer oven and air-fry for 12 minutes, tossing every 4 minutes. Using a food thermometer, check to ensure the internal temperature of the meatballs is 165°F.

Zesty London Broil

Servings: 4
Cooking Time: 28 Minutes

Ingredients:

- ⅔ cup ketchup
- ¼ cup honey
- ¼ cup olive oil
- 2 tablespoons apple cider vinegar
- 2 tablespoons Worcestershire sauce
- 2 tablespoons minced onion
- ½ teaspoon paprika
- 1 teaspoon salt
- 1 teaspoon freshly ground black pepper
- 2 pounds London broil, top round or flank steak (about 1-inch thick)

Directions:

1. Combine the ketchup, honey, olive oil, apple cider vinegar, Worcestershire sauce, minced onion, paprika, salt and pepper in a small bowl and whisk together.
2. Generously pierce both sides of the meat with a fork or meat tenderizer and place it in a shallow dish. Pour the marinade mixture over the steak, making sure all sides of the meat get coated with the marinade. Cover and refrigerate overnight.
3. Preheat the toaster oven to 400°F.
4. Transfer the London broil to the air fryer oven and air-fry for 28 minutes, depending on how rare or well done you like your steak. Flip the steak over halfway through the cooking time.
5. Remove the London broil from the air fryer oven and let it rest for five minutes on a cutting board. To serve, thinly slice the meat against the grain and transfer to a serving platter.

Pork Cutlets With Almond-lemon Crust

Servings: 3

Cooking Time: 14 Minutes

Ingredients:

- ¾ cup Almond flour
- ¾ cup Plain dried bread crumbs (gluten-free, if a concern)
- 1½ teaspoons Finely grated lemon zest
- 1¼ teaspoons Table salt
- ¾ teaspoon Garlic powder
- ¾ teaspoon Dried oregano
- 1 Large egg white(s)
- 2 tablespoons Water
- 3 6-ounce center-cut boneless pork loin chops (about ¾ inch thick)
- Olive oil spray

Directions:

1. Preheat the toaster oven to 375°F .
2. Mix the almond flour, bread crumbs, lemon zest, salt, garlic powder, and dried oregano in a large bowl until well combined.
3. Whisk the egg white(s) and water in a shallow soup plate or small pie plate until uniform.
4. Dip a chop in the egg white mixture, turning it to coat all sides, even the ends. Let any excess egg white mixture slip back into the rest, then set it in the almond flour mixture. Turn it several times, pressing gently to coat it evenly. Generously coat the chop with olive oil spray, then set aside to dip and coat the remaining chop(s).
5. Set the chops in the air fryer oven with as much air space between them as possible. Air-fry undisturbed for 12 minutes, or until browned and crunchy. You may need to add 2 minutes to the cooking time if the machine is at 360°F.
6. Use kitchen tongs to transfer the chops to a wire rack. Cool for a few minutes before serving.

Ribeye Steak With Blue Cheese Compound Butter

Servings: 2

Cooking Time: 12 Minutes

Ingredients:

- 5 tablespoons unsalted butter, softened
- ¼ cup crumbled blue cheese 2 teaspoons lemon juice
- 1 tablespoon freshly chopped chives
- Salt & freshly ground black pepper, to taste
- 2 (12 ounce) boneless ribeye steaks

Directions:

1. Mix together butter, blue cheese, lemon juice, and chives until smooth.
2. Season the butter to taste with salt and pepper.
3. Place the butter on plastic wrap and form into a 3-inch log, tying the ends of the plastic wrap together.
4. Place the butter in the fridge for 4 hours to harden.
5. Allow the steaks to sit at room temperature for 1 hour.
6. Pat the steaks dry with paper towels and season to taste with salt and pepper.
7. Insert the fry basket at top position in the Cosori Smart Air Fryer Toaster Oven.
8. Preheat the toaster Oven to 450°F.
9. Place the steaks in the fry basket in the preheated oven.
10. Select the Broil function, adjust time to 12 minutes, and press Start/Pause.
11. Remove when done and allow to rest for 5 minutes.
12. Remove the butter from the fridge, unwrap, and slice into ¾-inch pieces.
13. Serve the steak with one or two pieces of sliced compound butter.

Albóndigas

Servings: 4
Cooking Time: 15 Minutes

Ingredients:
- 1 pound Lean ground pork
- 3 tablespoons Very finely chopped trimmed scallions
- 3 tablespoons Finely chopped fresh cilantro leaves
- 3 tablespoons Plain panko bread crumbs (gluten-free, if a concern)
- 3 tablespoons Dry white wine, dry sherry, or unsweetened apple juice
- 1½ teaspoons Minced garlic
- 1¼ teaspoons Mild smoked paprika
- ¾ teaspoon Dried oregano
- ¾ teaspoon Table salt
- ¼ teaspoon Ground black pepper
- Olive oil spray

Directions:
1. Preheat the toaster oven to 400°F.
2. Mix the ground pork, scallions, cilantro, bread crumbs, wine or its substitute, garlic, smoked paprika, oregano, salt, and pepper in a bowl until the herbs and spices are evenly distributed in the mixture.
3. Lightly coat your clean hands with olive oil spray, then form the ground pork mixture into balls, using 2 tablespoons for each one. Spray your hands frequently so that the meat mixture doesn't stick.
4. Set the balls in the air fryer oven so that they're not touching, even if they're close together. Air-fry undisturbed for 15 minutes, or until well browned and an instant-read meat thermometer inserted into one or two balls registers 165°F.
5. Use a nonstick-safe spatula and kitchen tongs for balance to gently transfer the fragile balls to a wire rack to cool for 5 minutes before serving.

VEGETABLES AND VEGETARIAN

Roasted Root Vegetables With Cinnamon

Servings: 4
Cooking Time: 20 Minutes

Ingredients:

- 1 small sweet potato, cut into 1-inch pieces
- 2 carrots, cut into 1-inch pieces
- 2 parsnips, cut into 1-inch pieces
- 2 tablespoons brown sugar (dark or light)
- 1 tablespoon olive oil
- ¼ teaspoon ground cinnamon
- Oil spray (hand-pumped)
- Sea salt, for seasoning

Directions:

1. Preheat the toaster oven to 350°F on AIR FRY for 5 minutes.
2. In a large bowl, toss the sweet potato, carrots, parsnips, brown sugar, oil, and cinnamon until well mixed.
3. Place the air-fryer basket in the baking tray and generously spray the mesh with oil.
4. Spread the vegetables in the basket and air fry in position 2 for 20 minutes, shaking the basket after 10 minutes, until the vegetables are tender and lightly caramelized.
5. Season with salt and serve.

Empty-the-refrigerator Roasted Vegetables

Servings: 4
Cooking Time: 35 Minutes

Ingredients:

- 3 cups assorted fresh vegetables, cut into 1 × 1-inch pieces
- 2 garlic cloves, minced
- 2 tablespoons olive oil
- 3 tablespoons dry white wine
- Salt and freshly ground black pepper to taste
- 1 tablespoon chopped fresh basil
- 1 tablespoon chopped fresh oregano
- 1 tablespoon chopped fresh parsley

Directions:

1. Preheat the toaster oven to 400° F.
2. Combine all the ingredients with 2 tablespoons water in a 1-quart 8½ × 8½ × 4-inch ovenproof baking dish, mixing well. Cover the dish with aluminum foil.
3. BAKE, covered, for 25 minutes, until the vegetables are tender. Remove from the oven and stir to blend the vegetables and sauce.
4. BROIL, uncovered, for 10 minutes, or until lightly browned.

Fried Okra

Servings: 4
Cooking Time: 8 Minutes

Ingredients:
- 1 pound okra
- 1 large egg
- 1 tablespoon milk
- 1 teaspoon salt, divided
- ½ teaspoon black pepper, divided
- ¼ teaspoon paprika
- ¼ teaspoon thyme
- ½ cup cornmeal
- ½ cup all-purpose flour

Directions:
1. Preheat the toaster oven to 400°F.
2. Cut the okra into ½-inch rounds.
3. In a medium bowl, whisk together the egg, milk, ½ teaspoon of the salt, and ¼ teaspoon of black pepper. Place the okra into the egg mixture and toss until well coated.
4. In a separate bowl, mix together the remaining ½ teaspoon of salt, the remaining ¼ teaspoon of black pepper, the paprika, the thyme, the cornmeal, and the flour. Working in small batches, dredge the egg-coated okra in the cornmeal mixture until all the okra has been breaded.
5. Place a single layer of okra in the air fryer oven and spray with cooking spray. Air-fry for 4 minutes, toss to check for crispness, and cook another 4 minutes. Repeat in batches, as needed.

Homemade Potato Puffs

Servings: 4
Cooking Time: 15 Minutes

Ingredients:

- 1¾ cups Water
- 4 tablespoons (¼ cup/½ stick) Butter
- 2 cups plus 2 tablespoons Instant mashed potato flakes
- 1½ teaspoons Table salt
- ¾ teaspoon Ground black pepper
- ¼ teaspoon Mild paprika
- ¼ teaspoon Dried thyme
- 1¼ cups Seasoned Italian-style dried bread crumbs (gluten-free, if a concern)
- Olive oil spray

Directions:

1. Heat the water with the butter in a medium saucepan set over medium-low heat just until the butter melts. Do not bring to a boil.
2. Remove the saucepan from the heat and stir in the potato flakes, salt, pepper, paprika, and thyme until smooth. Set aside to cool for 5 minutes.
3. Preheat the toaster oven to 400°F. Spread the bread crumbs on a dinner plate.
4. Scrape up 2 tablespoons of the potato flake mixture and form it into a small, oblong puff, like a little cylinder about 1½ inches long. Gently roll the puff in the bread crumbs until coated on all sides. Set it aside and continue making more, about 12 for the small batch, 18 for the medium batch, or 24 for the large.
5. Coat the potato cylinders with olive oil spray on all sides, then arrange them in the air fryer oven in one layer with some air space between them. Air-fry undisturbed for 15 minutes, or until crisp and brown.
6. Gently dump the contents of the air fryer oven onto a wire rack. Cool for 5 minutes before serving.

Ranch Potatoes

Servings: 2
Cooking Time: 50 Minutes

Ingredients:

- 2 medium russet potatoes, scrubbed and cut lengthwise into ¼-inch strips
- 1 medium onion, chopped
- 2 tablespoons vegetable oil
- 2 tablespoons barbecue sauce
- ¼ teaspoon hot sauce
- Salt and freshly ground black pepper

Directions:

1. Preheat the toaster oven to 400° F.
2. Combine all the ingredients in a medium bowl, mixing well and adjusting the seasonings to taste.
3. Place equal portions of the potatoes on two 12 × 12-inch squares of heavy-duty aluminum foil. Fold up the edges of the foil to form a sealed packet and place on the oven rack.
4. BAKE for 40 minutes, or until the potatoes are tender. Carefully open the packet and fold back the foil.
5. BROIL 10 minutes, or until the potatoes are browned.

Roasted Cauliflower With Garlic And Capers

Servings: 3

Cooking Time: 10 Minutes

Ingredients:

- 3 cups (about 15 ounces) 1-inch cauliflower florets
- 2 tablespoons Olive oil
- 1½ tablespoons Drained and rinsed capers, chopped
- 2 teaspoons Minced garlic
- ¼ teaspoon Table salt
- Up to ¼ teaspoon Red pepper flakes

Directions:

1. Preheat the toaster oven to 375°F .
2. Stir the cauliflower florets, olive oil, capers, garlic, salt, and red pepper flakes in a large bowl until the florets are evenly coated.
3. When the machine is at temperature, put the florets in the pan, spreading them out to as close to one layer as you can. Air-fry for 10 minutes, tossing once to get any covered pieces exposed to the air currents, until tender and lightly browned.
4. Dump the contents of the air fryer oven into a serving bowl or onto a serving platter. Cool for a minute or two before serving.

Roasted Veggie Kebabs

Servings: 4
Cooking Time: 45 Minutes

Ingredients:
- Brushing mixture:
- 3 tablespoons olive oil
- 1 tablespoon soy sauce
- 1 teaspoon garlic powder
- 1 teaspoon ground cumin
- 2 tablespoons balsamic vinegar
- Salt and freshly ground black pepper to taste
- Cauliflower, zucchini, onion, broccoli, bell pepper, mushrooms, celery, cabbage, beets, and the like, cut into approximately 2 × 2-inch pieces

Directions:
1. Preheat the toaster oven to 400° F.
2. Combine the brushing mixture ingredients in a small bowl, mixing well. Set aside.
3. Skewer the vegetable pieces on 4 9-inch metal skewers and place the skewers lengthwise on a broiling rack with a pan underneath.
4. BAKE for 40 minutes, or until the vegetables are tender, brushing with the mixture every 10 minutes.
5. BROIL for 5 minutes, or until lightly browned.

Cauliflower

Servings: 4
Cooking Time: 6 Minutes

Ingredients:

- ½ cup water
- 1 10-ounce package frozen cauliflower (florets)
- 1 teaspoon lemon pepper seasoning

Directions:

1. Pour the water into air fryer oven.

2. Pour the frozen cauliflower into the air fryer oven and sprinkle with lemon pepper seasoning.

3. Air-fry at 390°F for approximately 6 minutes.

Wilted Brussels Sprout Slaw

Servings: 4
Cooking Time: 18 Minutes

Ingredients:
- 2 Thick-cut bacon strip(s), halved widthwise (gluten-free, if a concern)
- 4½ cups (about 1 pound 2 ounces) Bagged shredded Brussels sprouts
- ¼ teaspoon Table salt
- 2 tablespoons White balsamic vinegar
- 2 teaspoons Worcestershire sauce (gluten-free, if a concern)
- 1 teaspoon Dijon mustard (gluten-free, if a concern)
- ¼ teaspoon Ground black pepper

Directions:
1. Preheat the toaster oven to 375°F .
2. When the machine is at temperature, lay the bacon strip halves in the air fryer oven in one layer and air-fry for 10 minutes, or until crisp.
3. Use kitchen tongs to transfer the bacon pieces to a wire rack. Put the shredded Brussels sprouts in a large bowl. Drain any fat from the pan or the tray under the pan onto the Brussels sprouts. Add the salt and toss well to coat.
4. Put the Brussels sprout shreds in the air fryer oven, spreading them out into as close to an even layer as you can. Air-fry for 8 minutes, tossing the air fryer oven's contents at least three times, until wilted and lightly browned.
5. Pour the contents of the air fryer oven into a serving bowl. Chop the bacon and add it to the Brussels sprouts. Add the vinegar, Worcestershire sauce, mustard, and pepper. Toss well to blend the dressing and coat the Brussels sprout shreds. Serve warm.

Lemon-glazed Baby Carrots

Servings: 4

Cooking Time: 33 Minutes

Ingredients:

- Glaze:
- 1 tablespoon margarine
- 2 tablespoons lemon juice
- 1 tablespoon honey
- 1 teaspoon garlic powder
- Salt and freshly ground black pepper to taste
- 2 cups peeled baby carrots (approximately 1 pound)
- 1 tablespoon chopped fresh parsley or cilantro

Directions:

1. Place the glaze ingredients in a 1-quart 8½ × 8½ × 4-inch ovenproof baking dish and broil for 4 minutes, or until the margarine is melted. Remove from the oven and mix well. Add the carrots and toss to coat. Cover the dish with aluminum foil.
2. BAKE, covered, at 350° F. for 30 minutes, or until the carrots are tender. Garnish with chopped parsley or cilantro and serve immediately.

Baked Stuffed Acorn Squash

Servings: 2
Cooking Time: 25 Minutes

Ingredients:

- Stuffing:
- ¼ cup multigrain bread crumbs
- 1 tablespoon olive oil
- ¼ cup canned or frozen thawed corn
- 2 tablespoons chopped onion
- 1 teaspoon capers
- 1 teaspoon garlic powder
- Salt and freshly ground black pepper
- 1 medium acorn squash, halved and seeds scooped out

Directions:

1. Preheat the toaster oven to 400° F.
2. Combine the stuffing ingredients and season to taste. Fill the squash cavities with the mixture and place in an oiled or nonstick 8½ × 8½ × 2-inch square baking (cake) pan.
3. BAKE for 25 minutes, or until the squash is tender and the stuffing is lightly browned.

Fried Eggplant Slices

Servings: 3
Cooking Time: 12 Minutes

Ingredients:
- 1½ sleeves (about 60 saltines) Saltine crackers
- ¾ cup Cornstarch
- 2 Large egg(s), well beaten
- 1 medium (about ¾ pound) Eggplant, stemmed, peeled, and cut into ¼-inch-thick rounds
- Olive oil spray

Directions:
1. Preheat the toaster oven to 400°F. Also, position the rack in the center of the oven and heat the oven to 175°F.
2. Grind the saltines, in batches if necessary, in a food processor, pulsing the machine and rearranging the saltine pieces every few pulses. Or pulverize the saltines in a large, heavy zip-closed plastic bag with the bottom of a heavy saucepan. In either case, you want small bits of saltines, not just crumbs.
3. Set up and fill three shallow soup plates or small pie plates on your counter: one for the cornstarch, one for the beaten egg(s), and one for the pulverized saltines.
4. Set an eggplant slice in the cornstarch and turn it to coat on both sides. Use a brush to lightly remove any excess. Dip it into the beaten egg(s) and turn to coat both sides. Let any excess egg slip back into the rest, then set the slice in the saltines. Turn several times, pressing gently to coat both sides evenly but not heavily. Coat both sides of the slice with olive oil spray and set it aside. Continue dipping and coating the remaining slices.
5. Set one, two, or maybe three slices in the pan. There should be at least ½ inch between them for proper air flow. Air-fry undisturbed for 12 minutes, or until crisp and browned.
6. Use a nonstick-safe spatula to transfer the slice(s) to a large baking sheet. Slip it into the oven to keep the slices warm as you air-fry more batches, as needed, always transferring the slices to the baking sheet to stay warm.

DESSERTS

Honey-roasted Mixed Nuts

Servings: 8
Cooking Time: 15 Minutes

Ingredients:
- ½ cup raw, shelled pistachios
- ½ cup raw almonds
- 1 cup raw walnuts
- 2 tablespoons filtered water
- 2 tablespoons honey
- 1 tablespoon vegetable oil
- 2 tablespoons sugar
- ½ teaspoon salt

Directions:
1. Preheat the toaster oven to 300°F.
2. Lightly spray an air-fryer-safe pan with olive oil; then place the pistachios, almonds, and walnuts inside the pan and place the pan inside the air fryer oven.
3. Air-fry for 15 minutes, every 5 minutes to rotate the nuts.
4. While the nuts are roasting, boil the water in a small pan and stir in the honey and oil. Continue to stir while cooking until the water begins to evaporate and a thick sauce is formed. The sauce should stick to the back of a wooden spoon when mixed. Turn off the heat.
5. Remove the nuts from the air fryer oven (cooking should have just completed) and spoon the nuts into the stovetop pan. Use a spatula to coat the nuts with the honey syrup.
6. Line a baking sheet with parchment paper and spoon the nuts onto the sheet. Lightly sprinkle the sugar and salt over the nuts and let cool in the refrigerator for at least 2 hours.
7. When the honey and sugar have hardened, store the nuts in an airtight container in the refrigerator.

Baked Apple

Servings: 4
Cooking Time: 20 Minutes

Ingredients:
- 3 small Honey Crisp or other baking apples
- 3 tablespoons maple syrup
- 3 tablespoons chopped pecans
- 1 tablespoon firm butter, cut into 6 pieces

Directions:
1. Put ½ cup water in the drawer of the air fryer oven.
2. Wash apples well and dry them.
3. Split apples in half. Remove core and a little of the flesh to make a cavity for the pecans.
4. Place apple halves in air fryer oven, cut side up.
5. Spoon 1½ teaspoons pecans into each cavity.
6. Spoon ½ tablespoon maple syrup over pecans in each apple.
7. Top each apple with ½ teaspoon butter.
8. Preheat the toaster oven to 360°F and air-fry for 20 minutes, until apples are tender.

Carrot Cake

Servings: 6
Cooking Time: 30 Minutes

Ingredients:

- FOR THE CAKE
- ½ cup canola oil, plus extra for greasing the baking dish
- 1 cup all-purpose flour, plus extra for dusting the baking dish
- 1 cup granulated sugar
- 1 teaspoon baking powder
- ½ teaspoon sea salt
- 2 teaspoons pumpkin pie spice
- 2 large eggs
- 1 cup carrot, finely shredded
- ½ cup dried apricot, chopped
- FOR THE ICING
- 4 ounces cream cheese, room temperature
- ¼ cup salted butter, room temperature
- 1 teaspoon vanilla extract
- 2 cups confectioners' sugar

Directions:

1. To make the cake
2. Place the rack in position 1 and preheat the oven to 325°F on BAKE for 5 minutes.
3. Lightly grease an 8-inch-square baking dish with oil and dust with flour.
4. Place the rack in position 1.
5. In a large bowl, stir the flour, sugar, baking powder, salt, and pumpkin pie spice.
6. Make a well in the center and add the oil and eggs, stirring until just combined. Add the carrot and apricot and stir until well mixed.
7. Transfer the batter to the baking dish and bake for about 30 minutes until golden brown and a toothpick inserted in the center comes out clean.
8. Remove the cake from the oven and cool completely in the baking dish.
9. To make the icing
10. When the cake is cool, whisk the cream cheese, butter, and vanilla until very smooth and blended. Add the confectioners' sugar and whisk until creamy and thick, about 2 minutes.
11. Ice the cake and serve.

Dark Chocolate Banana Bread

Servings: 8
Cooking Time: 60 Minutes

Ingredients:

- ½ cup salted butter, melted, plus extra for greasing the pan
- 1 cup all-purpose flour, plus extra for dusting the pan
- ¾ cup dark brown sugar
- ¼ cup cocoa powder
- 2 teaspoons baking powder
- ¼ teaspoon sea salt
- 2 large bananas, mashed
- 1 large egg
- 1½ teaspoons vanilla extract
- ½ cup dark chocolate chips

Directions:

1. Place the rack in position 1 and preheat the oven to 325°F on BAKE for 5 minutes.
2. Grease a 9-by-5-inch loaf pan with melted butter and dust with all-purpose flour. Set aside.
3. In a medium bowl, stir the flour, brown sugar, cocoa powder, baking powder, and salt together until well combined.
4. In a medium bowl, whisk the butter, bananas, egg, and vanilla until well blended.
5. Add the wet ingredients to the dry ingredients and stir until combined. Add the chocolate chips and stir until incorporated.
6. Bake for 1 hour, or until a toothpick inserted into the center of the bread comes out mostly clean. If the bread starts to get too dark, cover the top with foil and bake until done.
7. Let the bread cool for 10 minutes and then run a knife around the edge and remove the bread from the loaf pan to cool completely on a rack.
8. Serve when cool.

Fried Snickers Bars

Servings: 8
Cooking Time: 4 Minutes

Ingredients:
- ⅓ cup All-purpose flour
- 1 Large egg white(s), beaten until foamy
- 1½ cups (6 ounces) Vanilla wafer cookie crumbs
- 8 Fun-size (0.6-ounce/17-gram) Snickers bars, frozen
- Vegetable oil spray

Directions:
1. Preheat the toaster oven to 400°F.
2. Set up and fill three shallow soup plates or small pie plates on your counter: one for the flour, one for the beaten egg white(s), and one for the cookie crumbs.
3. Unwrap the frozen candy bars. Dip one in the flour, turning it to coat on all sides. Gently stir any excess, then set it in the beaten egg white(s). Turn it to coat all sides, even the ends, then let any excess egg white slip back into the rest. Set the candy bar in the cookie crumbs. Turn to coat on all sides, even the ends. Dip the candy bar back in the egg white(s) a second time, then into the cookie crumbs a second time, making sure you have an even coating all around. Coat the covered candy bar all over with vegetable oil spray. Set aside so you can dip and coat the remaining candy bars.
4. Set the coated candy bars in the pan with as much air space between them as possible. Air-fry undisturbed for 4 minutes, or until golden brown.
5. Remove the pan from the machine and let the candy bars cool in the pan for 10 minutes. Use a nonstick-safe spatula to transfer them to a wire rack and cool for 5 minutes more before chowing down.

Peach Cobbler

Servings: 4
Cooking Time: 35 Minutes

Ingredients:
- FOR THE FILLING
- 4 cups chopped fresh peaches
- ½ cup sugar
- 2 tablespoons cornstarch
- 1 teaspoon vanilla extract
- FOR THE COBBLER
- 1 cup all-purpose flour
- ¼ cup sugar
- ¾ teaspoon baking powder
- Pinch of sea salt
- 3 tablespoons cold salted butter, cut into ½-inch cubes
- ½ cup buttermilk

Directions:
1. To make the filling
2. In a medium bowl, toss together the peaches, sugar, cornstarch, and vanilla.
3. Transfer to an 8-inch-square baking dish. Set aside.
4. To make the cobbler
5. Place the rack in position 1 and preheat the toaster oven to 350°F on BAKE for 5 minutes.
6. In a large bowl, stir the flour, sugar, baking powder, and sea salt.
7. Using your fingertips, rub the butter into the flour mixture until the mixture resembles coarse crumbs.
8. Add the buttermilk in a thin stream to the flour crumbs, tossing with a fork until a sticky dough forms.
9. Scoop the batter by tablespoons and dollop it on the peaches, spacing the mounds out evenly and leaving gaps for the steam to escape.
10. Bake for 35 minutes, or until the cobbler is golden brown and the filling is bubbly.
11. Serve warm.

Dark Chocolate Peanut Butter S'mores

Servings: 4
Cooking Time: 6 Minutes

Ingredients:

- 4 graham cracker sheets
- 4 marshmallows
- 4 teaspoons chunky peanut butter
- 4 ounces dark chocolate
- ½ teaspoon ground cinnamon

Directions:

1. Preheat the toaster oven to 390°F. Break the graham crackers in half so you have 8 pieces.
2. Place 4 pieces of graham cracker on the bottom of the air fryer oven. Top each with one of the marshmallows and bake for 6 or 7 minutes, or until the marshmallows have a golden brown center.
3. While cooking, slather each of the remaining graham crackers with 1 teaspoon peanut butter.
4. When baking completes, carefully remove each of the graham crackers, add 1 ounce of dark chocolate on top of the marshmallow, and lightly sprinkle with cinnamon. Top with the remaining peanut butter graham cracker to make the sandwich. Serve immediately.

Sweet Potato Donut Holes

Servings: 18
Cooking Time: 4 Minutes

Ingredients:
- 1 cup flour
- ⅓ cup sugar
- ¼ teaspoon baking soda
- 1 teaspoon baking powder
- ⅛ teaspoon salt
- ½ cup cooked mashed purple sweet potatoes
- 1 egg, beaten
- 2 tablespoons butter, melted
- 1 teaspoon pure vanilla extract
- oil for misting or cooking spray

Directions:
1. Preheat the toaster oven to 390°F.
2. In a large bowl, stir together the flour, sugar, baking soda, baking powder, and salt.
3. In a separate bowl, combine the potatoes, egg, butter, and vanilla and mix well.
4. Add potato mixture to dry ingredients and stir into a soft dough.
5. Shape dough into 1½-inch balls. Mist lightly with oil or cooking spray.
6. Place 9 donut holes in air fryer oven, leaving a little space in between. Air-fry for 4 minutes, until done in center and lightly browned outside.
7. Repeat step 6 to cook remaining donut holes.

Fried Oreos

Servings: 12
Cooking Time: 7 Minutes

Ingredients:
- 1 Large egg white(s)
- 2 tablespoons Water
- 1 cup Graham cracker crumbs
- 12 Original-size Oreos (not minis or king-size)
- Vegetable oil spray

Directions:
1. Preheat the toaster oven to 375°F .
2. Set up and fill two shallow soup plates or small pie plates on your counter: one for the egg white(s), whisked with the water until foamy; and one for the graham cracker crumbs.
3. Dip a cookie in the egg white mixture, turning several times to coat well. Let any excess egg white mixture slip back into the rest, then set the cookie in the crumbs. Turn several times to coat evenly, pressing gently. You want an even but not thick crust. However, make sure that the cookie is fully coated and that the filling is sealed inside. Lightly coat the cookie on all sides with vegetable oil spray. Set aside and continue dipping and coating the remaining cookies.
4. Set the coated cookies in the oven with as much air space between them as possible. Air-fry undisturbed for 6 minutes, or until the coating is golden brown and set. If the machine is at 360°F, the cookies may need 1 minute more to cook and set.
5. Use a nonstick-safe spatula to transfer the cookies to a wire rack. Cool for at least 5 minutes before serving.

Lime Cheesecake

Servings: 6
Cooking Time: 30 Minutes

Ingredients:
- Oil spray (hand-pumped)
- ½ cup graham cracker crumbs
- 24 ounces cream cheese, room temperature
- 1½ cups granulated sugar
- 4 large eggs
- ¼ cup sour cream
- Juice and zest of 1 lime
- 2 teaspoons vanilla extract

Directions:
1. Place the rack in position 1 and preheat the oven to 350°F on BAKE for 5 minutes.
2. Lightly spray an 8-inch springform pan with the oil and spread the graham cracker crumbs in the bottom.
3. Bake for 10 minutes, then remove the crust from the air fryer and set it aside.
4. In a large bowl, beat the cream cheese until very smooth with an electric hand beater. Add the sugar by ½-cup measures, beating very well after each addition and scraping down the sides of the bowl.
5. Add the eggs one at a time, beating well after each addition and scraping down the sides of the bowl.
6. Beat in the sour cream, lime juice, lime zest, and vanilla until very well blended and fluffy, about 4 minutes.
7. Transfer the batter to the pan and smooth the top.
8. Bake for 30 minutes or until set.
9. Let the cheesecake cool in the oven for 30 minutes and then transfer to the refrigerator to cool completely. Serve.

Orange Strawberry Flan

Servings: 4

Cooking Time: 45 Minutes

Ingredients:
- ¼ cup sugar
- ½ cup concentrated orange juice
- 1 12-ounce can low-fat evaporated milk
- 3 egg yolks
- 1 cup frozen strawberries, thawed and sliced, or 1 cup fresh strawberries, washed, stemmed, and sliced
- 4 fresh mint sprigs

Directions:
1. Preheat the toaster oven to 375° F.
2. Place the sugar in a baking pan and broil for 4 minutes, or until the sugar melts. Remove from the oven, stir briefly, and pour equal portions of the caramelized sugar into four 1-cup-size ovenproof dishes. Set aside.
3. Blend the orange juice, evaporated milk, and egg yolks in a food processor or blender until smooth. Transfer the mixture to a medium bowl and fold in the sliced strawberries. Pour the mixture in equal portions into the four dishes.
4. BAKE for 45 minutes, or until a knife inserted in the center comes out clean. Chill for several hours. The flan may be loosened by running a knife around the edge and inverted on individual plates or served in the dishes. Garnish with fresh mint sprigs.

Coconut Rice Pudding

Servings: 6
Cooking Time: 55 Minutes

Ingredients:
- ½ cup short-grain brown rice
- Pudding mixture:
- 1 egg, beaten
- 1 tablespoon cornstarch
- ½ cup fat-free half-and-half
- ½ cup chopped raisins
- 1 teaspoon vanilla extract
- ½ teaspoon ground cinnamon
- ½ teaspoon grated nutmeg
- Salt to taste
- ¼ cup shredded sweetened coconut
- Fat-free whipped topping

Directions:
1. Preheat the toaster oven to 400° F.
2. Combine the rice and 1½ cups water in a 1-quart 8½ × 8½ × 4-inch ovenproof baking dish. Cover with aluminum foil.
3. BAKE, covered, for 45 minutes, or until the rice is tender. Remove from the oven and add the pudding mixture ingredients, mixing well.
4. BAKE, uncovered, for 10 minutes, or until the top is lightly browned. Sprinkle the top with coconut and chill before serving. Top with fat-free whipped topping.

LUNCH AND DINNER

Pea Soup

Servings: 6

Cooking Time: 55 Minutes

Ingredients:
- 1 cup dried split peas, ground in a blender to a powderlike consistency
- 3 strips lean turkey bacon, uncooked and chopped
- ¼ cup grated carrots
- ¼ cup grated celery
- 2 tablespoons grated onion
- ½ teaspoon garlic powder
- Salt and freshly ground black pepper to taste
- Garnish:
- 2 tablespoons chopped fresh chives

Directions:
1. Preheat the toaster oven to 400° F.
2. Combine all the ingredients in a 1-quart 8½ × 8½ × 4-inch ovenproof baking dish, mixing well. Adjust the seasonings.
3. BAKE, covered, for 35 minutes. Remove from the oven and stir.
4. BAKE, covered, for another 20 minutes, or until the soup is thickened. Ladle the soup into individual soup bowls and garnish each with chopped fresh chives.

Baked Tomato Casserole

Servings: 4
Cooking Time:45 Minutes

Ingredients:

- Casserole mixture:
- 1 medium onion, coarsely chopped
- 3 medium tomatoes, coarsely chopped
- 1 medium green pepper, coarsely chopped
- 2 garlic cloves, minced
- ½ teaspoon crushed oregano
- ½ teaspoon crushed basil
- 1 tablespoon extra virgin olive oil
- 2 tablespoons chopped fresh cilantro
- Salt and freshly ground black pepper
- 3 4 tablespoons grated Parmesan cheese
- ¼ cup multigrain bread crumbs

Directions:

1. Preheat the toaster oven to 400° F.
2. Combine the casserole mixture ingredients in a 1-quart 8½ × 8½ × 4-inch ovenproof baking dish. Adjust the seasonings to taste and cover with aluminum foil.
3. BAKE, covered, for 35 minutes, or until the tomatoes and pepper are tender. Remove from the oven, uncover, and sprinkle with the bread crumbs and Parmesan cheese.
4. BROIL for 10 minutes, or until the topping is lightly browned.

Parmesan Artichoke Pizza

Servings: 6
Cooking Time: 15 Minutes

Ingredients:
- CRUST
- ¾ cup warm water (110°F)
- 1 ½ teaspoons active dry yeast
- ¼ teaspoon sugar
- 1 tablespoon olive oil
- 1 teaspoon table salt
- ⅓ cup whole wheat flour
- 1 ½ to 1 ⅔ cups bread flour
- TOPPINGS
- 2 tablespoons olive oil
- 1 teaspoon Italian seasoning
- 1 clove garlic, minced
- ½ cup whole milk ricotta cheese, at room temperature
- ⅔ cup drained, chopped marinated artichokes
- ¼ cup chopped red onion
- 3 tablespoons minced fresh basil
- ½ cup shredded Parmesan cheese
- ⅓ cup shredded mozzarella cheese

Directions:

1. Make the Crust: Place the warm water, yeast, and sugar in a large mixing bowl for a stand mixer. Stir, then let stand for 3 to 5 minutes or until bubbly.

2. Stir in the olive oil, salt, whole wheat flour, and 1 ½ cups bread flour. If the dough is too sticky, stir in an additional 1 to 2 tablespoons bread flour. Beat with the flat (paddle) beater at medium-speed for 5 minutes (or knead by hand for 5 to 7 minutes or until the dough is smooth and elastic). Place in a greased large bowl, turn the dough over, cover with a clean towel, and let stand for 30 to 45 minutes, or until starting to rise.

3. Stir the olive oil, Italian seasoning, and garlic in a small bowl; set aside.

4. Preheat the toaster oven to 450°F. Place a 12-inch pizza pan in the toaster oven while it is preheating.

5. Turn the dough onto a lightly floured surface and pull or roll the dough to make a 12-inch circle. Carefully transfer the crust to the hot pan.

6. Brush the olive oil mixture over the crust. Spread the ricotta evenly over the crust. Top with the artichokes, red onions, fresh basil, Parmesan, and mozzarella. Bake for 13 to 15 minutes, or until the crust is golden brown and the cheese is melted. Let stand for 5 minutes before cutting.

Roasted Vegetable Gazpacho

Servings: 4
Cooking Time: 35 Minutes

Ingredients:

- Vegetables and seasonings:
- 1 bell pepper, thinly sliced
- ½ cup chopped celery
- ½ cup frozen or canned corn
- 1 medium onion, thinly sliced
- 1 small yellow squash, cut into 1-inch slices
- 1 small zucchini, cut into 1-inch slices
- 3 garlic cloves, chopped
- ½ teaspoon ground cumin
- 2 tablespoons olive oil
- Salt and freshly ground black pepper to taste
- 1 quart tomato juice
- 1 tablespoon lemon juice
- 3 tablespoons chopped fresh cilantro

Directions:

1. Preheat the toaster oven to 400°F.
2. Combine the vegetables and seasonings in an oiled or nonstick 8½ × 8½ × 2-inch square baking (cake) pan, mixing well.
3. BAKE, covered, for 25 minutes, or until the onions and celery are tender. Remove from the oven, uncover, and turn the vegetable pieces with tongs.
4. BROIL for 10 minutes, or until the vegetables are lightly browned. Remove from the oven and cool. Transfer to a large nonaluminum container and add the tomato juice, lemon juice, and cilantro. Adjust the seasonings.
5. Chill, covered, for several hours, preferably a day or two to enrich the flavor of the stock.

Italian Baked Stuffed Tomatoes

Servings: 4
Cooking Time: 30 Minutes

Ingredients:

- 4 large tomatoes
- 1 cup shredded chicken
- 1 1/2 cup shredded mozzarella, divided
- 1 1/2 cup cooked rice
- 2 tablespoon minced onion
- 1/4 cup grated parmesan cheese
- 1 tablespoon dried Italian seasoning
- salt
- pepper
- Basil

Directions:

1. Preheat the toaster oven to 350°F. Spray toaster oven pan with nonstick cooking spray.
2. Cut the top off each tomato and scoop centers out. Place bottoms on prepared pan. Chop 3 tomatoes (about 1 1/2 cup, chopped) and add to large bowl.
3. Add shredded chicken, 1 cup shredded mozzarella cheese, rice, onion, Parmesan cheese, Italian seasoning, salt and pepper to large bowl and stir until blended. Divide between tomatoes, about 1 cup per tomato. Top with remaining mozzarella and tomato top.
4. Bake 25 to 30 minutes until cheese is melted and mixture is heated through.
5. Garnish with basil before serving.

One-step Classic Goulash

Servings: 4
Cooking Time: 56 Minutes

Ingredients:
- 1 cup elbow macaroni
- 1 cup (8-ounce can) tomato sauce
- 1 cup very lean ground round or sirloin
- 1 cup peeled and chopped fresh tomato
- ½ cup finely chopped onion
- 1 teaspoon garlic powder
- Salt and freshly ground black pepper
- Topping:
- 1 cup homemade bread crumbs
- 1 tablespoon margarine

Directions:
1. Preheat the toaster oven to 400° F.
2. Combine all the ingredients, except the topping, with 2 cups water in a 1-quart 8½ × 8½ × 4-inch ovenproof baking dish and mix well. Adjust the seasonings to taste. Cover with aluminum foil.
3. BAKE, covered, for 50 minutes, or until the macaroni is cooked, stirring after 25 minutes to distribute the liquid. Uncover, sprinkle with bread crumbs, and dot with margarine.
4. BROIL for 6 minutes, or until the topping is lightly browned.

Italian Stuffed Zucchini Boats

Servings: 6
Cooking Time: 26 Minutes

Ingredients:
- 6 small zucchini, halved lengthwise
- 1 pound bulk hot sausage
- 1 small onion, chopped
- 2 cloves garlic, minced
- 1 small Roma tomato, seeded and chopped
- 1/4 cup Parmesan cheese
- 3 tablespoons tomato paste
- 2 teaspoons dried Italian seasoning
- 1 teaspoon salt
- 1/2 teaspoon coarse black pepper
- 1 cup shredded mozzarella cheese
- Sliced fresh basil

Directions:
1. Preheat the toaster oven to 350°F. Spray a 13x9-inch baking pan with nonstick cooking spray.
2. Scoop out center of zucchini halves. Reserve 1 1/2 cups. Place zucchini boats in baking pan.
3. In a large skillet over medium-high heat, cook sausage, stirring to crumble, about 6 minutes or until browned. Remove sausage to a medium bowl.
4. Add onion and garlic to skillet, cook until onion is translucent. Stir in reserved zucchini, sausage, tomatoes, Parmesan cheese, tomato paste, Italian seasoning, salt and black pepper.
5. Spoon mixture into the zucchini boats.
6. Bake for 20 minutes. Remove from oven and top with mozzarella cheese.
7. Bake an additional 5 to 6 minutes or until cheese is melted.
8. Sprinkle with sliced fresh basil before serving.

Parmesan Crusted Tilapia

Servings: 2
Cooking Time: 14 Minutes

Ingredients:

- 2 ounces Parmesan cheese
- 1/4 cup Italian seasoned Panko bread crumbs
- 1/2 teaspoon Italian seasoning
- 1/4 teaspoon ground black pepper
- 1 tablespoon mayonnaise
- 2 tilapia fillets or other white fish fillets (about 4 ounces each)

Directions:

1. Preheat the toaster oven to 425°F. Spray baking pan with nonstick cooking spray.
2. Using a spiralizer, grate Parmesan cheese and place in a large resealable plastic bag. Add Panko bread crumbs, Italian seasoning and black pepper. Seal and shake bag.
3. Spread mayonnaise on both sides of fish fillets. Add fish to bag and shake until coated with crumb mixture.
4. Press remaining crumbs from bag onto fish. Place on prepared baking pan.
5. Bake until fish flakes easily with a fork, 12 to 14 minutes.

Dijon Salmon With Green Beans Sheet Pan Supper

Servings: 2-3

Cooking Time: 15 Minutes

Ingredients:

- 3/4 pound salmon fillets, cut in portion-size pieces
- 2 tablespoons olive oil
- 1 tablespoon soy sauce
- 1 tablespoon Dijon mustard
- 2 cloves garlic
- 6 ounces thin green beans, trimmed
- 1/2 small red bell pepper, thinly sliced
- 1/2 small yellow bell pepper, thinly sliced
- 1 small leek, white part only, thinly sliced
- Dash coarse black pepper

Directions:

1. Place rack on bottom position of toaster oven. Preheat the toaster oven to 400°F. Spray the toaster oven baking pan with nonstick cooking spray or line the pan with nonstick aluminum foil. Place salmon skin-side down in center of pan.
2. In a food chopper, process olive oil, soy sauce, mustard and garlic until blended and garlic is chopped. Set aside.
3. In a large bowl, combine green beans, bell peppers and leeks. Add 2 tablespoons olive oil mixture and stir until vegetables are coated. Arrange vegetables evenly in pan around salmon.
4. Drizzle salmon with remaining olive oil mixture.
5. Bake until salmon is done to medium-well and vegetables are crisp-tender, about 15 minutes.

Creamy Roasted Pepper Basil Soup

Servings: 4
Cooking Time: 35 Minutes

Ingredients:

- 1 5-ounce jar roasted peppers, drained ½ cup fresh basil leaves
- 1 cup fat-free half-and-half
- 1 cup skim milk
- 2 tablespoons reduced-fat cream cheese
- 1 teaspoon garlic powder
- 1 teaspoon paprika
- Salt and freshly ground black pepper to taste
- 2 tablespoons chopped fresh basil leaves (garnish for cold soup)
- 2 tablespoons grated Parmesan cheese (topping for hot soup)

Directions:

1. Preheat the toaster oven to 400° F.
2. Process all the ingredients in a blender or food processor until smooth. Transfer the mixture to a 1-quart 8½ × 8½ × 4-inch ovenproof baking dish.
3. BAKE, covered, for 35 minutes. Ladle into individual soup bowls and serve.

Healthy Southwest Stuffed Peppers

Servings: 6
Cooking Time: 30 Minutes

Ingredients:

- 1 tablespoon oil
- 1 small onion, chopped
- 1 garlic clove, minced
- 1/2 pound ground turkey
- 1/2 cup drained black beans
- 1/2 cup whole kernel corn
- 1 jar (16 oz.) medium salsa, divided
- 1/2 cup cooked white rice
- 1/2 teaspoon chili powder
- 1/2 teaspoon salt
- 1/4 teaspoon ground cumin
- 1/4 teaspoon black pepper
- 3 medium peppers, halved lengthwise leaving stem on, seeded
- 1/3 cup shredded Monterey Jack cheese, divided
- Sour cream
- Chopped fresh cilantro

Directions:

1. Preheat the toaster oven to 350°F. Spray baking pan with nonstick cooking spray.
2. In a large skillet over medium-high, heat oil. Add onion and garlic, cook for 2 to 3 minutes.
3. Add turkey to skillet, cook, stirring frequently, for 6 to 8 minutes or until turkey is cooked through.
4. Stir black beans, corn, 1/2 cup salsa, rice, chili powder, salt, cumin and pepper into turkey mixture.
5. Fill each pepper half with turkey mixture, dividing mixture evenly among peppers.
6. Top each pepper half with remaining salsa.
7. Bake 20 minutes. Sprinkle with cheese and bake an additional 10 minutes or until heated through.
8. Top with sour cream and cilantro.

Sage, Chicken + Mushroom Pasta Casserole

Servings: 6
Cooking Time: 35 Minutes

Ingredients:

- Nonstick cooking spray
- 8 ounces bow-tie pasta, uncooked
- 4 tablespoons unsalted butter
- 8 ounces button or white mushrooms, sliced
- 3 tablespoons all-purpose flour
- Kosher salt and freshly ground black pepper
- 2 cups whole milk
- ½ cup dry white wine
- 2 tablespoons minced fresh sage
- 1 ½ cups chopped cooked chicken
- 1 cup shredded fontina, Monterey Jack, or Swiss cheese
- ½ cup shredded Parmesan cheese

Directions:

1. Preheat the toaster oven to 350°F. Spray a 2-quart baking pan with nonstick cooking spray.
2. Cook the pasta according to the package directions; drain and set aside.
3. Melt the butter in a large skillet over medium-high heat. Add the mushrooms and cook, stirring frequently, until the liquid has evaporated, 7 to 10 minutes. Blend in the flour and cook, stirring constantly, for 1 minute. Season with salt and pepper. Gradually stir in the milk and wine. Cook, stirring constantly, until the mixture bubbles and begins to thicken. Remove from the heat. Stir in the sage, cooked pasta, chicken, and fontina. Season with salt and pepper.
4. Spoon into the prepared pan. Cover and bake for 25 to 30 minutes. Uncover, sprinkle with the Parmesan, and bake for an additional 5 minutes or until the cheese is melted.
5. Remove from the oven and let stand for 5 to 10 minutes before serving.

RECIPES INDEX

A

Albóndigas 70

Apple Maple Pudding 11

Apple Rollups 41

B

Baked Apple 84

Baked Asparagus Fries 39

Baked Stuffed Acorn Squash 81

Baked Tomato Casserole 96

Baked Tomato Pesto Bluefish 24

Barbecue-style London Broil 65

Beef Bourguignon 61

Beer-baked Pork Tenderloin 64

Better-than-chinese-take-out Pork Ribs 59

Blackened Red Snapper 21

C

Calf's Liver 60

Carrot Cake 85

Cauliflower 78

Chicken Breast With Chermoula Sauce 54

Chicken Pot Pie 53

Chicken Potpie 49

Chicken-fried Steak With Gravy 50

Coconut Jerk Shrimp 20

Coconut Rice Pudding 94

Coffee Cake 16

Cranberry Pecan Rice Pilaf 32

Creamy Bacon + Almond Crostini 14

Creamy Roasted Pepper Basil Soup 105

Creamy Scalloped Potatoes 37

Crispy Spiced Chickpeas 35

Crunchy Clam Strips 26

D

Dark Chocolate Banana Bread 86

Dark Chocolate Peanut Butter S'mores 89

Dijon Salmon With Green Beans Sheet Pan Supper 104

E

Empty-the-refrigerator Roasted Vegetables 72

F

Foolproof Baked White Rice 43

French Vegetable Tartines 12

Fried Chicken 56

Fried Eggplant Slices 82

Fried Okra 73

Fried Oreos 91

Fried Snickers Bars 87

G
Granola 13
Grilled Dagwood 17
Guiltless Bacon 45

H
Harissa Lemon Whole Chicken 55
Healthy Southwest Stuffed Peppers 106
Homemade Potato Puffs 74
Honey-roasted Mixed Nuts 83
Hot Italian-style Sub 9

I
Italian Baked Stuffed Tomatoes 100
Italian Meatballs 66
Italian Rice Balls 40
Italian Stuffed Zucchini Boats 102

L
Lemon-glazed Baby Carrots 80
Lemon-roasted Salmon Fillets 29
Lightened-up Breaded Fish Filets 30
Lime And Cumin Lamb Kebabs 58
Lime Cheesecake 92

M
Mediterranean Baked Fish 27
Mushroom-spinach Frittata With Feta 15

O
Oat Bran Muffins 18
One-step Classic Goulash 101
Orange Strawberry Flan 93
Oven-crisped Chicken 52
Oven-crisped Fish Fillets With Salsa 25

P
Parmesan Artichoke Pizza 97
Parmesan Crusted Tilapia 103
Parmesan Peas 38
Pea Soup 95
Peach Cobbler 88
Pork Cutlets With Almond-lemon Crust 68

Q
Quick Shrimp Scampi 23

R
Ranch Potatoes 75
Ribeye Steak With Blue Cheese Compound Butter 69
Roasted Cauliflower With Garlic And Capers 76
Roasted Root Vegetables With Cinnamon 71
Roasted Vegetable Gazpacho 99
Roasted Veggie Kebabs 77
Rotisserie-style Chicken 46

S
Sage Butter Roasted Butternut Squash With Pepitas 36
Sage, Chicken + Mushroom Pasta Casserole 107
Sesame-crusted Tuna Steaks 31
Smokehouse-style Beef Ribs 63
Spiced Sea Bass 22
Spicy Pigs In A Blanket 34
Stuffed Baked Red Snapper 28
Sweet And Spicy Pumpkin Scones 19
Sweet Potato Donut Holes 90
Sweet-and-sour Chicken 47

T
Tasty Meat Loaf 44
Thick-crust Pepperoni Pizza 33
Turkey Bacon Dates 42
Turkey-hummus Wraps 57

W
Wilted Brussels Sprout Slaw 79

Y
Yogurt Bread 10

Z
Zesty London Broil 67

Ingram Content Group UK Ltd.
Milton Keynes UK
UKHW051520290523
422514UK00012B/174